Praise for *Little Sprouts and*

"Drawing from the best of Chinese us antidotes to offset the intense pressures we face by showing us how to cultivate awareness, inquisitiveness, and empathy in the details of everyday life—birthday parties, walks, and even technology."
—Becky Yang Hsu, coeditor of *The Chinese Pursuit of Happiness*

"A deeply inspiring work about what classical Chinese philosophy can teach us about the art of parenting. This is a book that should be read and taken seriously by all parents and by anyone interested in nurturing the generations to come."
—Michael Puett, coauthor of *The Path*

"Erin Cline illustrates an ancient wisdom on the craft of parenting, which is not about being a soccer mom or a tiger mom, but flowing with the Dao. We nurture our little sprouts to grow and fill their own beautiful pots."
—Robin R. Wang, author of *Yinyang*

"Erin Cline has produced a profoundly personal, powerful, insightful, and elegant study showing how classical Chinese thought can help us nurture and raise more mindful, aware, intelligent, and compassionate children. This is a brilliant book, overflowing with wisdom, solidly grounded in classical sources that are astutely and creatively applied to a broad range of contemporary cases."
—Philip J. Ivanhoe, author of *Confucian Reflections*

Ancient Chinese Philosophy
and the Art of Raising
Mindful, Resilient,
and
Compassionate Kids

LITTLE SPROUTS
and the
Dao of Parenting

ERIN CLINE

W. W. NORTON & COMPANY
Independent Publishers Since 1923

Copyright © 2020 by Erin Cline

All rights reserved
Printed in the United States of America
First published as a Norton paperback 2021

For information about permission to reproduce selections from
this book, write to Permissions, W. W. Norton & Company, Inc.,
500 Fifth Avenue, New York, NY 10110

For information about special discounts for bulk purchases,
please contact W. W. Norton Special Sales at
specialsales@wwnorton.com or 800-233-4830

Manufacturing by Lake Book
Book design by Brooke Koven
Production manager: Anna Oler

Library of Congress Cataloging-in-Publication Data

Names: Cline, Erin M., author.
Title: Little sprouts and the Dao of parenting : ancient Chinese
philosophy and the art of raising mindful, resilient, and
compassionate kids / Erin Cline.
Description: New York, NY : W. W. Norton & Company, [2020] |
Includes bibliographical references and index.
Identifiers: LCCN 2019044491 | ISBN 9780393652314
(hardcover) | ISBN 9780393652321 (epub)
Subjects: LCSH: Tao. | Philosophy, Chinese. | Parenting.
Classification: LCC B127.T3 C55 2020 | DDC 649/.1—dc23
LC record available at https://lccn.loc.gov/2019044491

ISBN 978-0-393-54151-9 pbk.

W. W. Norton & Company, Inc.
500 Fifth Avenue, New York, N.Y. 10110
www.wwnorton.com

W. W. Norton & Company Ltd.
15 Carlisle Street, London W1D 3BS

1 2 3 4 5 6 7 8 9 0

*In loving memory of my father, Michael Slater Cline,
and for my mother, Dorothy Roberts Cline, with love*

A tree whose girth fills one's embrace sprang from a downy sprout;
A terrace nine stories high arose from a layer of dirt;
A journey of a thousand leagues began with a single step.

—THE *Daodejing*

Contents

A Note on Pronunciation

Two of the Chinese philosophers who are discussed in this book have especially difficult names to pronounce for many Western speakers. The Confucian philosopher Xunzi's name is pronounced "Shoon-zuh." The Daoist philosopher Zhuangzi's name is pronounced "Joo-awng-zuh."

LITTLE SPROUTS
and the
Dao of Parenting

Introduction

A tree whose girth fills one's embrace once sprang from a downy sprout.

——THE *Daodejing*

In general, having these sprouts within oneself, if one knows to fill them all out, it will be like a fire starting up, a spring breaking through. . . . If one delights in them then they grow. If they grow then how can they be stopped? If they cannot be stopped, then without realizing it one's feet begin to step in time to them and one's hands dance according to their rhythms.

——MENCIUS

Inch by inch, row by row, gonna make this garden grow.
All it takes is a rake and a hoe and a piece of fertile ground.[1]

——AMERICAN FOLK SONG

From my seat by the window on a bus in rural China, a voice next to me woke me from my thoughts. "You are an American student. You have come here to study Chinese?" I turned and my eyes met the twinkling eyes of an elderly Chinese woman who was smiling at me. "Yes," I replied, explaining that this was my first time visiting China, on a study abroad trip. She leaned back in her seat and smiled. "Okay," she said. "We will be friends." Then she said, "First, we will tell each other our life stories. You go first." *Um, okay,* I thought. *This will be interesting.* And I began, "Well, I was born in Homer, Alaska, which is where I grew up." I went on to talk about my love of music, growing up performing bluegrass and traditional Irish music, which is why I came to college as a music major. It didn't take that long to review my twenty-year-old life. But when I turned to my new friend and said, "There. Now, tell me about your life," I was in for a surprise. She leaned back in her seat and smiled. "My great-grandfather was an official in the Qing dynasty," she began, launching into a discussion of her great-grandfather's life. The story was fascinating, but I was filled with embarrassment. I had clearly misunderstood her question. *I was supposed to tell her about my family history, and I only talked about myself!* As I silently chastised myself for what I thought was a miscommunication due to language skills (I had just begun studying Chinese), she moved on to the lives of each of her other great-grandparents. I nearly interrupted her to apologize and explain, but it seemed rude. Her stories were remarkable. I was astonished at how much she knew about her great-grandparents, and her grandparents—not just the places they'd lived and the things they'd done, but the things that brought them joy, their strengths and weaknesses—*who they were* as people. As she worked her way down the family tree, telling me stories about each person, eventually getting to her parents and her husband's parents, and to her childhood, it hit me: she *is* telling me her story! I hadn't misunderstood. Her story *is* the story of her great-grandparents, her grandparents, her husband's grandparents and parents—at least, that is where it begins, from her perspective. Not with her birth, but with theirs. And I sat there, amazed at how differently she conceived of herself, of her own identity and of who she was, compared with how I viewed myself.

Who am I? Of all the questions philosophers ask, this is surely the most basic. But until that moment, it had always struck me as utterly abstract and, frankly, not of much practical value. But because of that bus ride, I came to see how you might think about yourself very differently from how I did—and how that might make a big difference in how you live. It would lead me to study with scholars who showed me that for ancient Confucian philosophers, our relationships and our place within a family are central to who we are—not a mere extension of it. It would also touch my life deeply on a personal level.

Twenty years after that conversation on the bus, I sat with my children in a church pew at my father's funeral, listening to my Uncle Tom's reflections on my dad's life. He paused and looked at us—my brother and I, our spouses, and my parents' seven grandchildren. "Look at that," he said, his blue eyes filling with tears. "What a legacy." And my mind raced back to that day on the bus, and the life story of my newfound Chinese friend. One of the things that made my friend's telling of her life story so *true* was that she grasped that she would not exist, nor would she be where she is or who she is, without the many choices of those who had gone before her. And so, too, does my father's story continue in the lives of his children and grandchildren—and one day, it will continue in the lives of his great-grandchildren.

I have devoted my career to teaching and studying Chinese philosophy; I am also a mother of three young children. Other parents often ask me whether Chinese philosophy has influenced my parenting. The answer? Absolutely, and in many different ways. They often go on to ask whether Chinese philosophers think we should all be tiger mothers. They are always taken aback, however, by my answer: it is hard to imagine a bigger contrast to the "tiger-mother" approach than the views of ancient Chinese philosophers. Perhaps this should not surprise us, since contemporary and ancient cultures differ in many ways. What *should* surprise us—and what has surprised me again and again as a parent and as a professor of Chinese philosophy—is that the lessons that ancient Chinese philosophers have for parents are so useful, accessible, and timely for parents today. Indeed, I find that they guide and challenge me on a daily basis, but in ways that depart—sometimes very dramatically—from what society tells us. My aim in this book is to help other parents—as well as grandparents, aunts, uncles, and all those who care for and nurture children—to benefit from these lessons as well.

In contrast to today's success-obsessed, achievement-oriented approaches to parenting, ancient Chinese philosophers contend that we should not strive for material wealth and prestige for our children, but to help them to become compassionate and generous people who make the world around them kinder, gentler, and more beautiful; only then will they truly be capable of flourishing as people. While they encourage us to help our children to be learned, this does not mean that they should be academic overachievers. The knowledge that they sought was thought to make them wiser, and better able to serve the world. This picture of human flourishing includes not only our basic well-being and happiness, but also finding genuine *fulfillment* in life—which, they argue, ultimately comes not from earning power or prestigious schools, but from loving and being loved by others within the context of meaningful, lasting relationships; understanding the way in which your own identity is bound up with the lives of those who have gone before you; giving generously of what you have to others; caring for and having a genuine love for nature; and finding your true vocation—no matter how humble it might be. Indeed, Chinese philosophers tell us that we should recognize and value many different kinds of vocations, gifts, and abilities (including different kinds of intelligence), not privileging one over the others. How can we help our children to flourish in these ways? This book describes the values and approaches that define Chinese philosophy, applying it to the daily lives and experiences of contemporary American parents and children and arguing that these ancient philosophers offer timeless wisdom for parents of all cultures.

FROM LITTLE SPROUTS TO FLOURISHING PLANTS

The ancient Chinese philosopher Mencius tells a story about a farmer who, day after day, went out into the field to check on the little sprouts growing there. He could see them stretching up out of the soil, little by little, day by day. But he grew impatient. He wanted them to grow taller and faster than the sprouts in the surrounding fields. One day, he decided to help his sprouts grow. He began tugging gently at the tender shoots, expecting them to stretch up a little higher with the push they needed. To his dismay, the first sprout he tugged at lifted right out of the soil, its tiny roots exposed to the sun. He tried another sprout, expecting it to be more deeply rooted, but the same thing happened. Again and again, no matter how gently he tugged, the sprouts ripped out of the ground as he tried to help them. "I'll replant them! I can repair the damage!" he declared. But despite his best efforts to tuck them gently back into the earth, when the farmer returned to his field the next day, all of his sprouts were withered.

Of all the colorful metaphors Chinese philosophers use, perhaps the most compelling is Mencius's metaphor of children as tender sprouts. They are shaped by so many different things: soil, sunlight, water, and, importantly, the efforts of patient farmers and gardeners. At times they require protection from weeds or a late spring frost, or when they are in danger of being trampled. At other times, what they most need is for us to take a step back and allow them to grow, for it is easy to harm them inadvertently. Unlike sprouts growing in untended fields and forests, the sprouts Mencius describes are planted in gardens and fields, where humans tend to them, just as our children who grow up in human communities. And as philosopher Philip J. Ivanhoe points out, Mencius intentionally chose the metaphor of sprouts, not seeds. For, like sprouts, a child's character, tendencies, virtues and vices—even from the earliest stages—are observable, not hidden; they are dynamic and changeable, not fixed.[2] Under the right conditions, sprouts can grow steadily and eventually flourish as strong, healthy plants. But what truly helps children to flourish, and what does it mean for a child—or an adult—to flourish like a healthy, flowering plant? In order to answer the most fundamental questions about parenting, Chinese philosophers believed we must explore some of the most challenging philosophical questions of all—questions about which Mencius and other ancient Chinese philosophers had much to say.

While countless recent books on parenting have examined the insights of other cultures, none has yet tapped the fascinating and surprising insights of ancient Chinese philosophers. Their insights are age-old and yet offer timely lessons for parents today. But they had a very different take on parenting than what many people associate with Chinese culture. One particularly well-known memoir presenting an extreme, success-obsessed "Chinese" approach to parenting by a Chinese American mother is emblematic of this view. Amy Chua's *Battle Hymn of the Tiger Mother* details her tough, no-holds-barred approach to parenting her two daughters, including how she threatened to burn her older daughter's stuffed animals if she didn't improve her piano playing, how she rejected the birthday cards her daughters had made for her because they were unimpressive (and ordered them to make better ones), and how she did not allow her daughters to have play dates or sleepovers, all in the service of raising them to be academic and musical overachievers—an approach she associates with being a Chinese mother.

While Chua always insisted that her book is a memoir, not a parenting manual, it prompted much curiosity about traditional Chinese approaches to parenting. It also highlighted a goal that many contemporary parents have: to help their children achieve in ways that are perceived to show that they are "extraordinary," or superior to others in certain ways. This goal reflects a particular (and very narrow) definition of success: one that is closely connected to certain types of academic achievements, how prestigious your college and chosen career are, and how much money you make. Indeed, these are widely and uncritically accepted as indicators of success by many parents today. And they are views that ancient Chinese philosophers wholly rejected.

Philosophers from the two most influential Chinese traditions—Confucianism and Daoism—both offer stinging indictments of the view that we should measure a person's success in these terms, instead offering a very different picture of success and human flourishing. To begin with, ancient Chinese philosophers talk more about human flourishing, virtue, happiness, and fulfillment than "success." This is because they recognized that often, those who lead the happiest, most fulfilling lives—those who *really flourish* as human beings—are not those who achieve *worldly* success, measured by wealth, prestige, and power. If they do possess these things, their happiness and flourishing seem to be *in spite of* it, not *because of* it. To clarify, it is not that Chinese philosophers disregarded the importance of material well-being; they wanted all children to be provided for (and to one day be able to provide for themselves and their families). But they knew there was a difference between the goals of providing for your family and having the highest earning power, and between being appreciated and valued, and enjoying prestige and power. Measuring success by money, prestige, and power, they believed, does not take into account the real marks of a successful life, or a life well lived. (At funerals, you never hear anyone remember or eulogize another by saying what his income was, how many cars or boats he had, or how he "crushed" the competition in his field of work.)

Chinese philosophers wrote a lot about reaching our full potential, which is why the metaphor of sprouts growing in a field was so important to them. This metaphor is not foreign to us. Indeed, it has universal appeal. Psychologist Alison Gopnik writes that "caring for children is like tending a garden, and being a parent is like being a gardener"—where we create nurturing space for plants to flourish in the midst of many uncertainties and surprises; in most cases, we never really have full control over the garden. Parenting is *not,* Gopnik argues, like being a carpenter, where "essentially your job is to shape the material into a final product that will fit the scheme you had in mind to begin with."[3] More than two thousand years earlier, Chinese philosophers used the metaphor of sprouts growing in fields in a number of additional ways, but they also used artisanal metaphors of carpenters, potters, wheelwrights, and cooks to illustrate some of the work of parenting. They, too, believed that parenting is messy, and that children's growth is ever-changing and often unpredictable; but this is why our work as parents sometimes resembles the task of a patient farmer, and other times the task of a determined artisan.

Most importantly, Chinese philosophers used these metaphors because they understood flourishing in *moral* terms: those who have truly realized their potential are those who have most fully cultivated virtues such as humaneness and compassion, and who have found their true calling or vocation in life, fulfilled in both their work and personal lives. This is like nurturing sprouts of grain so that they can grow into healthy stalks. And there *is* something the sprouts are meant to become. A barley sprout does not grow into a daisy. For Mencius, we have the "sprouts" or beginnings of virtues in us as children, and they are meant to develop into virtues like compassion and generosity—not only through the gardening efforts of parents, grandparents, aunts, uncles, friends and teachers, but also through our own efforts to nurture and realize our own moral potential as we grow. Chinese philosophers argued that we *genuinely flourish*—are happiest and most fulfilled—when we develop these virtues. Yet as Harvard professor Michael Puett points out—and as any parent knows—there is a lot that can go wrong. We may not give our sprouts enough water or nourishment, "or else we are too forceful: we grab them and try to tug at them to make them grow. Not only do we disrupt our natural goodness, but also we become miserable, easily dominated by our worst instincts: jealousy, anger, and resentment. When we do this, we harm our own humanity and harm those around us."[4] Something has been lost. Our potential has not been realized.

The sprout that grows into a flourishing plant is the child who fully realizes her potential. But this can *never* be measured in terms of things like earning power, attending prestigious schools, or having prestigious jobs. It is measured in how she treats people—how she loves and is loved by her family and friends—and in what she does to make the world a kinder, gentler, more humane, and beautiful place. The examples of admirable individuals described by ancient Chinese philosophers care deeply for their friends and family, for nature, and for society at large. They also possess a diverse array of talents, skills, and abilities: intellectual abilities are not privileged over the abilities of skilled artisans, carpenters, teachers, cooks, or butchers. Chinese philosophers challenge our understanding of intelligence and skill, pointing to forms of intelligence that are not measured by test scores. They challenge our view of education by insisting that developing a genuine *love* of learning is more important than how much (or how quickly) you learn.

BIG QUESTIONS FOR MODERN PARENTS

Ancient Chinese philosophers also challenge us in asking the biggest question of all: How do we judge the worth of a life? For parents, this boils down to the following question: What do we want most for our children? Chinese philosophers insist that although it is natural to want our children to realize their potential and cultivate their talents, skills, and abilities, our primary concern should be their happiness and virtue. We should want them to find their place in the world by doing something that brings joy and meaning to their lives and to the lives of others. These things—not wealth and prestige—will enable them to truly flourish and be fulfilled. These are the true marks of a life well lived.

Without question, this view is deeply at odds with contemporary achievement-oriented approaches to parenting commonly found in the United States and in many other parts of the modern world. (Many readers will be struck by the contrast between ancient Chinese philosophy and contemporary Chinese culture, as well as views that are prevalent in Asian American families. This book shows how different ancient and modern cultures can be.) Yet despite these contrasts, I believe the views of ancient Chinese philosophers resonate with the deepest desires of most parents. For when most of us reflect on what we most want for our children, it is to be happy and fulfilled, and to truly love and be loved by others. Readers will recognize some traditional East Asian values in this book, but they will also encounter some views that seem to transcend time and place. For instance, there are surprising resonances between the vision of a good life presented by ancient Chinese philosophers and a number of deeply held American beliefs and values—such as the democratic view that there is a rich diversity of good lives and that we ought to work to appreciate and value them, and the view that we should encourage individuals to develop their unique talents and abilities rather than encouraging conformity. The values of individuality, nonconformity, creativity, personal expression, and diversity are all at work in these texts, but often in unexpected ways.

For me, this is the most surprising insight of all: ancient Chinese philosophy suggests ways of living out some of our deepest values—but they are values that often conflict with the goals we tend to pursue without criticism. In this way, it offers advice to today's parents that is at once deeply countercultural and yet also in line with our deepest values and intuitions. Confucian and Daoist philosophers, each in their own way, urge us not to conform uncritically to what those around us are doing. The teachings of the most well-known and beloved philosophers from these traditions date to the third and fourth centuries BCE. They lived in a difficult time in Chinese society—a time of growing political instability, which eventually erupted into warfare and violence—but they disagreed on the source of the problem and how to fix it.

Confucian philosophers were inspired by the life and teachings of Confucius (551–479 BCE), who was the catalyst for virtually all of the philosophical debate and discussion that went on in ancient China. He is easily one of the most influential thinkers who ever lived—and perhaps *the* most influential thinker who ever lived, if we consider the influence of his teachings about the importance of family, respect for elders, learning, and ritual on the various cultures of East and Southeast Asia for the past 2,500 years. The philosopher Bryan Van Norden points out that if we imagined the *combined* influence of Jesus and Socrates on the Western tradition, we might begin to get a sense of Confucius's impact.[5] He started out holding some minor official posts—including serving as police commissioner—but decided he could make a bigger difference as a teacher and spent most of his life instructing his students and followers. Confucius believed that a cultural moral decline was the primary source of the problem with his society. He was concerned that people were beginning to neglect important rituals and social customs because they saw them as overly formal, unnecessary, and pointless. Confucius was convinced that these seemingly little practices—if done in the right way—are the very things that help us to become caring, grateful people and to lead meaningful lives—leading to harmonious relationships in families, in communities, and in the wider society. Confucian philosophers encourage us to focus on the meaning of rituals and the feelings they evoke, and to amend and adapt rituals and traditions to fit our own families, while also preserving and valuing them.

In contrast, Daoist philosophers—united by their belief in a guiding force known as the Dao, which is at work in the world and also beyond it—urge us to reject much of what our societies hand to us as the proper standards for a good life (including those rituals the Confucians thought were so important). Our society and culture, they believed, tend to pull us away from our original goodness and our original harmony with the Dao—harming us by telling us to work harder and become more. The Daoists thought we should embrace very different activities and goals—those that keep us close to the simple gifts of nature (and close to the Dao), and allow us each to develop our unique natural talents (which reflect our innate goodness), instead of conforming to the artificial goals our culture and society foist on us.

The diverse views on parenting that are found in Confucian and Daoist texts are precisely what make Chinese philosophy such a great resource for parents. Parenting is messy. It is not simple or straightforward but complex and difficult. There are no magic solutions that make everything (or even most things) easy or smooth. There are, however, better and worse ways of doing things, and ways that work better for some families but not others. Most of us will need to piece together different approaches in order to find something that works well and feels right in each situation, for individual children, and at particular times in a child's life. Fortunately for us, in addition to having different approaches, Chinese philosophers also wrote about different things, so in each chapter I present and draw upon the perspectives of a variety of philosophers on a wide range of topics, from special occasions like children's birthdays to spending time in nature, to finding your child's special talents and gifts, to how we view disabilities. For me, one of the great strengths in drawing upon the Chinese philosophical tradition is that it urges us to think hard about what we are doing, and why; to stick to traditions when they are meaningful and serve us well, and to innovate when they don't; and to avoid always conforming to what everyone else around us is doing. Instead, we must seek the way that is right for our own children and families, in all their individuality and all their distinctiveness.

Indeed, the Confucians and Daoists were a little like yin and yang, and that's why I think we need them both. Confucian philosophers believed that although children might have some good tendencies, it still takes a lot of support and hard work to grow into caring, compassionate people. In contrast, Daoist philosophers believed that we are born good, and that if we only followed our instincts and were allowed to develop naturally, without harmful interference, we would keep our original goodness. The Confucians have a lot of active, hands-on ways to help children grow, such as participating in rituals and traditions, while the Daoists recommend simpler, quieter activities, such as exploring and savoring the beauty of nature. I believe these two approaches can be complementary, and can help today's parents to achieve the right balance between providing support and allowing natural growth. They can help us to see when and how to step in and take a hands-on approach to children's development, and when to step back and let them grow. Just as yin and yang illustrate the necessary balance we need between things like darkness and light, Confucian and Daoist approaches point to the balance that children and parents need.

While they offer different insights, the Confucians and Daoists actually both believed in the idea of the Dao (道, "the Way"). Confucians understood it as being more like a path through life as opposed to the dynamic guiding force that the Daoists thought it was, but they shared the view that following the Dao means leading a truly fulfilling life, to flourish, and to be happy. Confucians and Daoists thought that following the Dao in parenting involves different kinds of activities, and they describe specific approaches to help us to live out that vision. They also describe a different way of *being with* our children. And their insights are sometimes startlingly progressive by modern standards. They celebrate the tireless work of dedicated single mothers; they highlight the importance of fathers showing their children affection; and they describe how parental love and care have a lasting impact on even the youngest infants, arguing that the earliest years of life play a critical role in shaping who we become. Utilizing that metaphor of sprouts growing in a field, they argued that the love, trust, and respect between parents and children are the "root" of the other virtues we can develop over the course of a lifetime. Today, developmental psychology tells us that they were right.

As a result of their belief in the importance of these early experiences, they not only wrote about the virtues that we ought to cultivate in our children, but they also developed ways to do it. Early Daoist views highlight the importance of encouraging children to spend free time in nature as a way of nurturing a love for the natural world and a commitment to caring for the environment—something that is more relevant for us today than ever before. Ancient Confucian philosophers, in turn, insisted on the importance of rituals, traditions, customs, and matters of etiquette. They believed that many of the simplest practices—like watching a friend open a gift we have chosen for her—can shape our children's character and help them to become kind, compassionate, and grateful people who are able to have meaningful, lasting relationships with others. But they also argued that in order for any of these practices to be helpful and meaningful, we must help our children to understand and reflect on *why* we do them. Only through reflection, attentiveness, and, they believed, mindfulness can we help our children to become the people we want them to be, and in the process, find ourselves changed for the better as well.

In the end, this emphasis on mindfulness and reflection is why Chinese philosophy offers such a profound source of inspiration and guidance: the insights of Chinese philosophers actually resonate with and awaken many of our deepest sensibilities as parents and our values. In spite of what we sometimes say and do, most of us really do care more about our children's happiness and well-being than the honors and recognition they receive from others or their future earning power. These texts can help us to evaluate our priorities and parent our children in ways that more accurately reflect our most deeply held beliefs, values, and goals. But while the ancient Chinese tradition has a variety of constructive resources for us, I want to emphasize that these values and goals are not uniquely Chinese. Every major religious tradition and the works of numerous philosophers throughout history emphasize the value of leading a happy, flourishing, virtuous life over the pursuit of wealth and prestige. Indeed, this is one of the reasons why most of us know "deep down" (by virtue of the different traditions and cultures that have informed our lives) that money and fame will not ultimately make us happy and are not the things we should seek as our ultimate goals in life. Yet as the ancient Daoist text the *Daodejing* says, "These are things everyone in the world knows but none can practice." Throughout history, wealth, prestige, and power have been seductive and alluring advantages across all human cultures, and we persist in being drawn to the pursuit of these things, partly because we do not adequately reflect on what we are doing and why. This is why Chinese philosophers urge us not to follow others uncritically, to think carefully about how we spend our time and why, and to reflect on what the aims and goals of our practices are—for all of these things can help us to shape our children into the kinds of people we really hope they will become.

❧ 1 ❧

Cultivated Sprouts
and the Dao of Rituals

Ritual encompasses the great and the small, the manifest and the subtle.

—*The Confucian Record of Ritual*

If I'm not fully present at a ritual, it's as if I haven't performed it at all.

—CONFUCIUS

wasn't expecting the American flag. As I stood on the snow-covered ground of an Alaskan cemetery that February day, balancing our two-year-old on my hip while our six-year-old daughter and nine-year-old son clutched each of my arms, I watched my husband, brother, and the other pallbearers slide my father's casket out of the back of a black Suburban. (They use Suburbans, not hearses, in Alaska.) I had known my father was a veteran, but that was all I could think of: I wasn't expecting my father's casket to be covered in an American flag. Truthfully, I hadn't expected my father's casket at all. He had died suddenly a week before. The men from the woodworking group at my parents' church had generously and lovingly made his casket from locally sourced wood not far from where I grew up, and that day I knew I would see the beautiful handmade casket. But I was taken aback by the sight of the flag.

At the funeral, my dad's cousin had talked about his military service. He had known my dad as a young man, when he joined the Air National Guard because he and his friends believed it was inevitable that they would be drafted, and figured that if they enlisted, they would at least be able to serve together. But though he reenlisted once, his unit was not called up before he completed his service. My dad went on to a career as an anthropologist and a schoolteacher, and he didn't talk about those years very often. But one of his cousin's fondest childhood memories was proudly watching my dad march in uniform with the other soldiers in a parade. An entire part of my father's story was revealed to me in the days following his death. That day, I was struck by two things: first, how rituals provide an opportunity to learn more about the people we love—even people we know very well; and second, I witnessed how rituals bind us to others—some who are present and some who are not present. As I watched my father's flag-draped casket make its way to his grave, I looked at my mother, knowing that the last time she had stood beside a flag-draped casket was the day of her brother's funeral. I thought of the families of veterans who mourn beside flag-draped caskets every year. I considered how our grief was connected, as though we were part of a family. I also felt gratitude, not only for my father's life, but also for the lives and sacrifices of all those to whom we are connected by that flag.

Chinese philosophers talk a lot about rituals. But they don't use the word "ritual" in the same way we do. In the ancient language in which the earliest Chinese philosophers wrote, the term for "ritual" (*li*, 禮) has a very broad semantic range. It takes many modern English words for us to capture all of the things they meant by it, including "rituals" as well as "social customs," "etiquette," and "manners." Confucian philosophers used the word "ritual" not just for things like funerals, baptisms, Bat Mitzvahs, and weddings, but also for things like shaking someone's hand and introducing yourself, writing thank-you notes, bringing a present to a birthday party, or having a big family meal on Thanksgiving Day.

Why did they call all of these things "rituals"? Well, one reason is that they thought we should take them more seriously than we do. After all, one of the things that distinguishes rituals from other practices is a certain degree of solemnity and respect. We take rituals more seriously than matters of etiquette or social customs. People in ancient China were starting to overlook and disregard a lot of those daily practices, seeing them as pointless, stuffy vestiges of the past. But Confucian philosophers urged people to take a closer look. What's in a handshake, a thank-you note, or a birthday gift? Much more than we think. Confucian philosophers believed that if we get the little things right—partly by thinking more about what we are doing and why, on occasions both large and small—it can change our lives. They also thought it would change *us*. And this is why they wanted us to find the sacred in the everyday, and to value and bring a sense of reverence to the little, seemingly insignificant things we do, just as we value more extravagant occasions.

Why are these rituals so important? Why do they matter to Chinese philosophers? As we have seen, the Confucian philosopher Mencius likened us to sprouts being cultivated in a field, and he and other Confucians viewed rituals as the water, sunshine, and nutrients in the soil. Like the rakes and hoes of gardeners and farmers, rituals are some of the most important tools for cultivating virtues and creating and maintaining meaningful relationships with others. This work is occurring through all sorts of daily rituals. When we teach our children to pause for a moment when an elevator door opens to let others exit before getting on, it certainly makes things more efficient and keeps people from getting upset because they had difficulty getting off the elevator. But by requiring us to look for others before charging ahead, this ritual can help us to become less self-centered and more attuned to the needs of others. It may seem unbelievable that such a minor practice can make this sort of difference, but just like plants are nurtured daily by a little water and a little sunlight, so too are our childrens' characters slowly being shaped by the rituals they learn—or fail to learn—from us.

Confucian philosophers argued that many different virtues are important—from compassion, respectfulness, and generosity to persistence, patience, and wisdom. They believed that all of these virtues are worth cultivating because they help us to lead richer, more fulfilling, happier lives. And they thought rituals offered a unique and powerful way of cultivating those virtues. Small, daily rituals (like saying please and thank-you, or letting people exit an elevator before you enter it)—along with rituals associated with special occasions (like birthdays, weddings, and funerals)—are one of the keys to helping our children to become kind, generous, and happy people. Since kids learn rituals from attentive parents, family members, friends, and teachers, Confucian philosophers have some important advice for us: think deeply about these practices, work to understand why and how they should be done, and make time to do them the right way with children. There is much more to them than it seems.

APPLYING CONFUCIAN INSIGHTS:
THE ART OF THANK-YOU NOTES

Chinese philosophers describe a wide range of virtues and relationships that are cultivated through a wide range of rituals (and remember, when we talk about rituals here, we mean many different types of practices). It is about why and how we have our children baptized or dedicated as infants, why and how we hold Bar or Bat Mitzvahs or quinceañeras. It is about what we do on our children's birthdays, why we do it, and how we do it. It is about what we do on Thanksgiving and other important holidays, and how we accompany our children through the joyful experiences of graduations and weddings, and the difficult experiences of funerals, wakes, or sitting shiva. But when we interpret "ritual" broadly, we also see the sacred in the everyday. This means finding meaning and opportunities for personal growth in the smallest details of our lives, and in apparently minor or perfunctory practices.

For example, while writing a thank-you note for a gift you have received may seem like it is solely for the person who gave you the gift, this practice is in fact for you as well, because it cultivates the virtue of generosity. Here's how it works. In order to write a meaningful thank-you note, you must take the time to reflect on what others have done for you or given you, what it required of them, and why you appreciate it. These actions cultivate a genuine sense of gratitude for the thoughtfulness, generosity, and sacrifice of others. When I write a thank-you note to my child's teacher, if I do it the Confucian way, I don't just hastily scrawl "Thank you! You're awesome!" on a card as I am about to dash out the door. Confucians would have me sit down and think about the specific things I have noticed about my child's teacher, and name them, describing what I have seen. When I do this, not only do I show the teacher that I have noticed her and let her know how grateful I am, I actually notice what she has done more fully myself, in the process of thinking and writing.

Although noticing and feeling grateful for the things others do for us contributes to our overall happiness on an ordinary day, it is especially important in difficult times. Sometimes, a simple practice that helps us to notice the sources of light in our lives—however small—can buoy our spirits in the midst of challenges. This is just as important for the teacher who receives a note as it is for the parent who writes it, and the child who delivers it to the teacher. Gratitude is particularly powerful in this way. A striking example is seen in the book *A Simple Act of Gratitude* by John Kralik, who details his experience after setting the goal of writing a thank-you note every single day for a year—a goal he set for himself only after hitting rock bottom and becoming desperate to change his life.

After deciding that his life might become more tolerable if he found a way to focus on what he had to be grateful for, rather than all of the ways his life seemed like a failure, he started writing thank-you notes to everyone from past business associates, college friends, and doctors to store clerks, handymen, and neighbors. In addition to touching the lives of many people whose work or gestures are often overlooked, no area of Kralik's life was left unchanged by what he did. He was thoroughly transformed by this practice, and his life was immeasurably better—*he* was immeasurably better.[1]

What does this have to do with children and parenting? Well, Confucians were keen to point out that we are not islands, even though we sometimes act like it. Chinese philosophers believed that if we parent our children in some of the ways they envisioned, not only our children will be transformed, but so also will we. Our growth is not wholly separate from theirs. Our children are often more affected by the things they see us doing—and the things we tell them we are doing—than by the things we tell them to do. So even if they aren't yet able to write a detailed thank-you note to a teacher, like we can, they are often influenced by our actions, especially if we take the time to share with them what we are doing and why, and allow them to participate, even in small ways like by drawing a picture or simply delivering the note. Rituals are transmitted to us little by little, step by step, and in the most miniscule ways. And even though young children cannot write the same note that a parent can, they can talk with us about the things that others have done for them. Rituals like writing thank-you notes not only teach us to express gratitude but also help us and our children to become more grateful people.

This act must be done collaboratively—children need support in this endeavor—but the power of ritual is especially pronounced in children, because they take to rituals quickly. Regularity and repetition are a key part of rituals, and children thrive on routines, which provide comfort through their reliability and also allow them to master something. Rituals also frequently involve expressing our feelings and thoughts, as well as sharing them with others—something else that children enjoy and benefit from. Indeed, kids are often sad to see one season and its rituals end, wishing to continue them into a new season. (My children would gladly observe Advent year-round, with the nightly lighting of the candles on our Christmas pyramid and the singing of our Advent song.)

At the same time, and in addition to making us more grateful (and therefore happier), rituals like writing thank-you notes offer us a powerful way of creating, nurturing, and maintaining meaningful relationships with others. To be sure, this works only if we engage in these practices in the right way: taking the time to do them carefully. It also works only if we recognize that practices like writing thank-you notes are about more than letting someone know that we are thankful for something they did or something they gave us. Writing a note is one way of continuing a relationship, beyond gift giving. Chinese philosophers knew that for most of us, it seems silly to make so much out of little things that we do and never think about—to the extent that we sometimes stop doing them because we think they don't really matter. We end up letting them fall by the wayside. But far from being insignificant, Confucius argued, these small practices are the stuff of our lives and the primary way in which we become better people and deepen our relationships with others.

Beyond telling us that we ought to see many different kinds of practices and occasions as rituals because they can make us more caring, grateful people, Confucian philosophers offer some interesting guidelines that challenge today's parents when it comes to our observance of rituals. They warn us about the temptation to use rituals to display or flaunt the things we have (such as material wealth). This is especially applicable to parties or celebrations of various kinds. They also warn us about worrying too much about how things look. In both of these cases, we become overly concerned with the material aspects of rituals, to the neglect of the meaning of rituals, and also to the neglect of being fully present at them. Yet the *Analects* tells us, "When it comes to ritual, better to be spare than extravagant." And "when it comes to mourning, better to be excessively sorrowful than fastidious."[2] In other words, it is better to have the right feelings about what you are doing—feelings that are appropriate to the occasion— than to be worried about how you look or how extravagant the gathering is, how perfect the tablecloth or the food. For Confucius, we are just forgetting what it is all about if we get caught up in those kinds of details.

Indeed, one of the two most important guidelines that Confucian philosophers offer us about rituals is that in order for rituals to make a difference in our lives, we need to understand their meaning and purpose. Confucius criticized those who did not understand the meaning behind rituals because the failure to understand their purpose made them pointless. For example, in ancient China, people usually bowed before ascending a set of stairs as a way of asking permission to enter and speak with someone. But people lost track of the meaning of the ritual and instead started bowing after they ascended the stairs. Confucius thought this made the whole ritual pointless, since one had already entered by the time one bowed; it would be like knocking on someone's door after you had already opened it and come inside. This is where we come in as parents: it's our job to teach children why certain rituals exist. For Confucius, this is the only way rituals can help make us better people.

The second guideline is that we need to be *fully present* in the things we do. The most influential Confucian text in history, *The Analects*, contains the following quote from Confucius: "If I am not fully present at a ritual, it's as if I haven't performed the ritual at all."[3] We can do things quickly or go through the motions without really thinking about it, or without our children's participation. Or we can do them attentively, viewing them as important opportunities for us and our children to stop and think about our relationships with others, what others have done for us, and why they are important to us. If I do the latter, I am fully present at the ritual, and that makes all the difference.

For children, there is a close relationship between understanding the meaning of rituals and being fully present at them. Before my dad's funeral, the adults in our family spent a lot of time talking with the grandchildren about why we have funerals, and how they give us a chance to cry, to share how sad we feel, and to remember someone we love—together with others who loved him (and who also love us). We also offered them the opportunity to participate in the service by sharing their memories, singing, and reading scripture verses. For my son, who loved birdwatching with my dad, we chose a Biblical reading from Isaiah 40:31 ("You shall mount up with wings as eagles . . .") and my mom added a picture of an eagle to the card he read from—which helped him to be more present at the ritual with us. He proudly held up the photograph for all to see after he finished reading his verse, and it hangs on his bedroom wall to this day, next to a picture of his grandfather.

THE CONFUCIAN ART OF NAMES, HOSTING, AND HANDSHAKES

Another ritual that Confucians took seriously is how we address people. From a Confucian perspective, calling your aunt not just by her first name but also by her title is a way to both show respect and be reminded of your special relationship to her and her distinctive position in the family. (In both ancient and modern Chinese, what you call your aunts and uncles differs according to their relationship to you and your parents; for instance, your mother's elder sister would have a different title than that for her younger sister.) Confucians thought this reflected and reminded us of reality: we really do have a wholly unique relationship with our parents, which is why we call them by a different name than anyone else. But they also thought it would help us to have better relationships with each other. On this view, when my undergraduate students call me Professor Cline, it should remind me of my responsibility to them, and when my graduate students call me by my first name, it should remind me that in addition to serving as their teacher, it is also my responsibility to help them become good colleagues. The things we say and do not only reflect what we think, but they also have the power to shape what we think.

When it comes to forms of address, there are many things for parents to consider. Whereas not too long ago in American culture, our children's friends would have called us "Mr." or "Mrs.," today it is a widespread practice in many regions of the country to use first names for adults. One day, a fellow parent remarked to me, "It just seems odd when a seven-year-old says, 'Hi Paul. Can Liam come over and play?' These days we're all pretty informal so kids call me 'Paul.' It's not wrong, but it doesn't feel quite right. But I've never had the guts to ask them to use 'Mister . . . .'" Confucius would point out that it doesn't feel quite right because it doesn't mirror the reality of the relationship: we have a responsibility to children who visit our homes, and this is unlike the relationship children have with each other. Culturally, as Americans, we are especially sensitive to abuses of authority and we tend to feel discomfort with inequalities, so we tend to think only of children showing respect through this practice. We want children to feel comfortable approaching us, and we don't want to look like we are on a "power trip" by having them address us more formally. These are worthy concerns, and they may be good reasons for us to have children address us by our first names.

But Confucius would point out that forms of address are just as important for adults as they are for children. While using different names can help to remind children to be respectful of adults (which is why most schools have children address teachers by "Mr." or "Ms."), it also helps to remind adults of the responsibility we have to children. Forms of address, in the Confucian tradition, were also designed to prevent certain relationships from being overly or inappropriately familiar. Using last names (family names) is also significant from a Confucian perspective. One of my friends insists that he doesn't like being called "Mr." because, as he puts it, "That's my dad, not me!" But Confucius would tell him that it's not such a bad thing to be reminded of your parents, and of our changing roles as we grow and age. Indeed, he might probe further about whether part of the discomfort here has to do with getting older. In our culture, we tend to want to be "forever young," and we go to great lengths to avoid aging or looking older. For Confucius, though, we should be grateful that we have the chance to assume the roles our parents once held. And when we are addressed using our last names, it should remind us that we are a part of a family and not just an individual. Ideally, it should remind us of the things our parents did for us and our friends growing up. It's an opportunity to learn from their example and from their mistakes, to be thoughtful about what we want to do differently and what we would like to pass on to our children. Even if it's just a fleeting moment of reflection, sometimes that's exactly what we need—a little nudge in the right direction. The memory of making homemade ice cream with friends who came over to play at our house nudges me to be a little more generous and fun, like my mom was, but it also reminds me that you can be equally fun and firm: if I think of my mom, I am more likely to make sure everyone helps clean up before they go home.

Forms of address aren't everything, of course: children can call adults by their first names and still be respectful, or call them by titles and be disrespectful, and adults can be called by titles and forget their responsibilities. But Confucius knew that language was a unique tool that can sometimes help us to do a little better by reminding us of who we are. Above all I think he would urge modern parents to think carefully about forms of address, and to see them as tools that are worth trying when it comes to helping our children—and us—to navigate relationships more successfully. I also think he would urge us not to be afraid to deviate from what everyone else is doing, whether that means forging new ground or recovering traditional practices that may have been discarded too quickly and uncritically. Confucius himself did this, as seen in the example discussed earlier of why bowing before ascending the stairs makes more sense than bowing after. As he put it, "These days people bow after ascending. But though it goes against the majority, I continue to bow before ascending."[4]

In thinking about our children's friends, how they address us, and our responsibilities to them, I cannot help but think of playtime—especially in the form of modern playdates. From a Confucian perspective, our children learn many rituals through playdates—or at least they should. Indeed, Confucius might worry about the fact that playtime is less frequent today, since children are enrolled in more activities. Learning to be a good guest, and learning to be a good host, is, after all, not completely straightforward, and most of the lessons are not just about being polite: they are also about good character. When we teach our children to give their guests priority when it comes to choosing what to play, they are getting practice in not being self-centered. The very best practice my kids get at compromise also occurs during playdates, and it requires significant coaching until they get the hang of it. (This is one example: Why does Emma want to play with our puppy? Because she doesn't have a puppy! Remember how excited you were to play with puppies before we had one?

Let's play with the puppy for a while, since she's our guest, and then we can do something else!)

Similarly, in preparing children to visit friends' homes, when we teach them how to politely ask for something or decline something that is offered when they visit someone's home—and *what* is appropriate to ask for (a glass of water, but not a meal)—they are learning how to be thoughtful of hosts. There are also important rituals for parents in relation to playdates, such as reciprocating: if someone hosts your child, the nice thing to do is invite their child over. We should want our children to get practice hosting friends, as well as being a guest. We should also want our children to observe in us an example of reciprocity and thoughtfulness that they can emulate. But while our children observe many of our actions and will pick some things up from watching us, they still need explicit instruction, and reminders, before they go to someone's house. I fully appreciated this only after having other children decline snacks we served at playdates by declaring that they hated that particular food, or ask for various other kinds of food instead. (This is a true story: one child told us steak was his favorite, and asked if we had some!) Confucius insisted that these are all opportunities for our children to become better people—they aren't just learning random rules of etiquette; they are learning to be thoughtful, kind, and grateful toward those who open up their home to you.

Even as my children have progressed in learning to host friends, I have been struck by just how complicated the learning process can be. For example, our family had established a rule that bigger kids who come to visit are not allowed to play on a small slide in our youngest daughter's room. But then my older daughter hosted a playdate, and she led her friend to the door of her sister's room, pointed at the slide, and announced, "You can't go on that slide. I can, but you're not allowed." *And then she slid down the slide in front of her friend.* Her friend shrugged it off, but afterward, we had a conversation with our daughter about how you shouldn't do something your guests can't do, and how it isn't necessary to bring up things that guests aren't allowed to do unless it seems like they are about to do them, and how it may be best to avoid little sister's room altogether on playdates in the future. Helping my kids learn about the rituals involved in hosting a friend involves a lot of conversations about empathy—imagining how you would feel if you were a guest at their house. It is very much about teaching our children to be thoughtful of others. And this is precisely why Confucius puts so much weight on teaching our children about rituals.

In guiding and instructing children on rituals, large and small, it can be an extraordinary experience to discover just how complex our rituals and social customs are. Instructing your children on matters of ritual, custom, and etiquette will lead you to be more attentive to what you are doing and accomplishing in these everyday exchanges. When I began to teach our son how to shake someone's hand (Don't grab their hand too hard, but not too loose, either!), I began to discover just how many elements of greeting someone were important. He had a tendency to grab someone's hand while looking around or at the floor, and I had to coach him, "Look them in the eyes as you shake their hand!" This is not something that would naturally occur to a child, nor are the particular things you say when you shake someone's hand—it must all be learned. But everything that goes into a handshake really hit home for us one day when our neighbors—good friends of ours from Korea—paid us a visit, with an urgent question: "In America, is it rude to have your other hand in your pocket when you shake someone's hand?" My husband and I both hesitated, puzzled by the question. Our friends then explained that Bill Gates had met the Korean president, and had shaken her hand while having his other hand in his pocket. This had caused an uproar among many Koreans and Korean Americans, who felt that he had been rude. After hearing this story and reflecting a bit, my husband and I explained that this wasn't really considered rude in America but that it was on the casual side, when it comes to handshakes—more like the kind of thing you'd do when meeting someone at a backyard barbecue. We tried to assure them that it was unlikely Bill Gates had intended to be rude. (Chalk it up to the more laid-back West Coast ethos, perhaps?) But we felt that there was something to the Korean sensibility here, and it led us to add a bit more instruction to our handshake lessons for our children: stand up straight, and hands out of pockets—especially if you're meeting a world leader!

THE CONFUCIAN ART OF BIRTHDAY PARTIES

If we focus more on the meaning of rituals—and reflect on why we do them—we will appreciate the importance of the many rituals that are a part of our families and communities. We will also look for opportunities to invest rituals with meaning. In other words, if we want rituals to help our children to become better people (and to help us become better people, too), then we should not only understand why certain rituals exist, but we should also look for ways to make them more meaningful.

When my children were in preschool and in the early years of elementary school, the practice of almost every other parent we knew was to invite the entire class (roughly twenty to twenty-five children) to a birthday party. This is an inclusive gesture with, I think, some very positive aims and motivations, such as cultivating friendships and making sure that no children feel excluded or have hurt feelings over not being invited. The problem is that few parents feel able to host such a large birthday party at their home (both due to the limitations of space and also because of the work involved in hosting so many children and parents). Therefore, the party is usually held at another location—typically an indoor children's recreational center. An entire industry thrives on this practice, at locations with all sorts of diversions for children.

(Gyms, dance studios, and karate studios have gotten in on the action as well.)

Since most of the families we knew were doing this, I felt pressure to do it, too. Yet we knew it was not the right choice for our family, for many reasons. It was very countercultural when we hosted a smaller party at home (even though, ironically, the party we hosted was more "traditional" in that it was similar to the parties we and our parents had growing up). One of our son's six-year-old friends even told him that you weren't "supposed" to have a birthday party at your home; you were "supposed" to have it at a fun place with bouncy castles or climbing walls. But we worked hard to put together fun parties for our kids, and the kids *did* have fun (and so did we). And for us, birthdays became an important moment in which we, as a family, said, "In our family, we do things *this* way. It's our tradition. We know it's different from what other people do. And we *are* different! But isn't every family different? And isn't that a good thing?" It became an opportunity to teach our children the meaning and value of tradition, on the one hand, and of individuality, on the other. This is a remarkable fusion: tradition and individuality. But for Confucian philosophers, this is precisely what rituals both large and small should be: carrying on traditions that have value but also making them our own.

Indeed, Chinese philosophers can offer considerable wisdom to today's parents concerning our tendency to uncritically conform to what others are doing, especially regarding changes to traditional rituals. This is a basic human tendency—it is not simply cultural, and I stress this because American culture is particularly known for being *more* individualistic and *less* prone to conformity than so many other cultures. When it comes to rituals, though, we have a tendency to conform too quickly. For example, our tendency is to want to host birthday parties for our children that are similar to those others are hosting. Even without overt peer pressure, we felt a certain compulsion to do this.

Confucius believed that we all need to get better at embracing the value of our own traditions. Growing up, I knew that my birthday cake would always be made by my mother, and that it would be carried on the same cake platter that had carried my father's birthday cakes and my grandmother's before him. Today, my children know the same thing. They are participating in family traditions that give them a sense of connection to the past and the present—traditions that teach them they are part of something much larger than themselves or our immediate family. Particularly in a society as beautifully diverse as the contemporary American one in which I live, rituals and traditions represent an opportunity for families to avoid conformity and develop their own individuality. This is good for all of our children: to see that you should not always do what everyone else is doing; to the contrary, you should take pride in your individuality. Surely, this sensibility represents the very best of American culture.

But when it comes to children's birthday parties, Confucius would worry about more than conformity; he would worry about the loss of several rituals that play an important role in children's lives. This may seem surprising, because we tend to view celebrations like birthday parties as nothing more than occasions for having fun. But Confucius was convinced that they are much more. Consider, for example, the ritual of having a child open gifts at her birthday party. This ritual has been eliminated from most parties my children have attended, because when one invites a large number of children, it takes too much time to open the gifts. So the gifts are usually dropped into a large bin, and that is the last that children see of the gift they gave. The gifts are opened later, at home. Sometimes thank-you notes are written, sometimes not (perhaps due to the large number of attendees and gifts).

Confucian philosophers would want us to notice what is lost here, and they would start with the meaning of the rituals. Why do we take a gift to a birthday party? What is the purpose of that ritual? Birthdays are an opportunity to give thanks to people we care about, and the ritual of gift giving at birthdays is an opportunity to do something to tell friends and family members that we care about them and that we are glad to have them in our lives. Of course, for children, birthday parties are occasions for having fun—playing games, eating favorite foods and treats. But giving a birthday gift is an example of a ritual that represents an opportunity, if we focus just a bit more on the purpose of the ritual. How involved are our children in choosing the gifts they take to birthday parties? How much time do we take to help them think about their friends and select something thoughtfully? Confucian philosophers see rituals such as gift giving as an opportunity that is often missed. It requires more time on our part to help our children do it thoughtfully, by brainstorming what their friend really likes, and then by shopping for— or making—together something that fits the bill. But when I do that, I've noticed that my children start to take joy in the task of finding something for a friend (instead of just for themselves).

They also look forward to their friend opening the gift, and they start to anticipate how happy it will make them. But children who attend birthday parties where gifts are not opened no longer have an opportunity to witness a friend opening the gift they chose—which can be an important step in learning about the joy of giving. (This is a long process for children, and that makes the experience of *seeing* a friend's joy at receiving a gift you gave them important.) Confucian philosophers viewed rituals holistically and communally, so Confucius would note the losses on all sides. Children who do not open gifts at their own birthday parties lose the chance to learn to express gratitude in person for gifts, and to learn the things that one should *not* say upon opening a gift (e.g., "I already have two of these!"), and why. In addition, other children miss the opportunity to learn by watching the gift-opening process. This experience is important: it is not always your moment to shine or to receive recognition, or to be the recipient of gifts, and you must learn to be a gracious and cheerful guest. From a Confucian perspective, this is not just a matter of children learning to *tolerate* occasions where they are not the center of attention; it is also a matter of learning to *enjoy* those occasions. Confucian philosophers argue that rituals don't just shape the character of those who are participating in them, but also those who witness them. Therefore, from a Confucian perspective, what happens when one child opens a gift given by another is complex and multifaceted: all of the children have an opportunity to learn a variety of things about generosity, gratitude, and friendship. But they aren't just learning lessons: they are developing feelings and attitudes, and getting practice at expressing those feelings and attitudes as they build relationships.

Now, some parents worry that it seems like bragging when one opens gifts at a birthday party, and that all of the other children will feel bad that they are not receiving gifts. This is a thoughtful motivation for wanting to eliminate gift opening at parties. But Confucian philosophers would argue that this is precisely why it is so important *not* to eliminate the ritual. Other children must learn not to feel bad when a child opens gifts on her birthday. In fact, wouldn't we like our children to be *happy* for her? And it's not just birthdays. Life is going to be filled with analogous circumstances. As an adult, we all witness colleagues and friends who win recognitions that we do not. How do we learn not to feel jealous and bitter when others receive attention and recognition and, yes, gifts, when we do not?

And how do we become people who genuinely find it easy to feel *happy for others*, and not just for ourselves—happy, for instance, to see others receive the recognition they so richly deserve? Well, those are all cultivated dispositions and attitudes. It is quite natural to feel jealousy and bitterness, and in order to not feel in these ways and to genuinely feel happy for others—which is ultimately something that affects our overall happiness—we must exercise those parts of ourselves, just like exercising a muscle. Birthday parties are one of the most frequent early opportunities we have to do that.

Interestingly, ancient Confucian philosophers argued that children should participate in rituals from the earliest years of their lives, and today just as in ancient China, our children are exposed to a wide range of rituals that can cultivate a variety of virtues in them—so long as we are aware of them and help to facilitate this process. But these rituals are not isolated from one another. Participating in the rituals that are a part of birthday parties as children prepares us for rituals that we will participate in as adults, such as wedding showers and baby showers. Adults at these showers usually enjoy watching the guests of honor open the gifts they picked out. And guests of honor typically express gratitude and joy as they open these gifts. It is important to remember that we don't magically develop the ability to respond to each other in these ways. Occasions such as birthday parties begin to shape us, as children, into gracious recipients of gifts, and into people who find joy in giving gifts to those we care about. But all of this can only happen if we support our children in seizing these opportunities for growth.

This is why Confucians urge us to use caution when we change or disregard rituals. Sometimes, there is hidden wisdom in traditions. Often, we don't notice that wisdom until it is gone. That is one more vote in favor of taking a Confucian approach and working to pay attention to what we are doing when we practice rituals (in the broad sense), why we do them and how they shape us. Even in Confucius's time, though, people tended to disregard rituals quickly, seeing them as unnecessary vestiges of the past. This is true for us today, too.

There are a number of things parents might reconsider when it comes to birthday parties. First, be intentional about having your child choose birthday gifts for friends. Have them spend a little time considering their friends' interests so that they can select something thoughtfully. Brainstorming of this sort can easily be done in the car or over dinner. Second, consider having your child open gifts at her birthday party. You may need to invite fewer children to make this manageable, but you may find that it is better for your child not to be inundated with gifts. Learn to see yourself as a coach in the process of gift opening, since there is a lot to learn. Third, spend some time thinking about how you do your children's parties and why, and how you can make them more meaningful occasions. Think about family traditions you enjoyed as a child and how you might incorporate them. Consider downsizing and welcoming your children's friends into your home.

View birthday parties as an opportunity to do something creative for and with your child and her friends. Have your child help choose a theme, and do some research for ideas. Parties can also be built around a group activity, regardless of age. Some friends of ours once had all the kids at their daughter's birthday party work together to solve the kidnapping of her favorite stuffed monkey. There was a ransom video with clues, and the kids went around the neighborhood hunting for more clues, interviewing neighbors, etc. When the same friends' daughter turned fifteen, she loved Audrey Hepburn movies. For that party, they hung a sheet in their back yard to serve as a movie screen, borrowed a projector from a friend, and transformed the space into an outdoor movie theater for their daughter and a small group of friends—who all dressed to the nines. My friend even dressed in black and white and served as their waiter, carrying a tray high over her head to serve the girls dinner. As her husband said later, "That one didn't take a whole lot of planning on our part, but it feels special to be outside in the dark watching a movie." From examples like this, we can glean another key piece of advice: view birthday parties as a fun and worthwhile investment of your time and energies. This is the most important invitation that Chinese philosophers make to us as parents: to be mindful of what we are doing to show our children we care about them. If we do this, we will find rewards not only for our children but for ourselves as well.

INNOVATING RITUALS, THE CONFUCIAN WAY

Partly as a result of the excessive readiness to disregard traditional rituals, we sometimes find ourselves in a world bereft of the rituals we and our children need. This was true when my cousin Brian died while I was in college. A year after his death, as our family prepared to accompany Brian's widow and two young children to visit his grave, my mother made a stunning observation: "We don't know what to do." Indeed, although there had been a clear path to follow in the weeks after Brian died—the memorial service, the burial, the steady visits from friends and family—there was no path to follow now. What were we to do when we got to the cemetery and found ourselves standing beside his gravestone? Our culture offered us nothing, except that we should take flowers to lay on his grave. Bereft of rituals to follow, I began thinking about the ancient Confucian rituals that had always seemed so foreign. I knew they all involved physical actions that were designed to stir the heart and mind with appropriate feelings and memories. Mourning rituals, which continued not for weeks but years, were supposed to give people not only an outlet for their grief but also an opportunity to remember the person they had lost and to continue to hold them in their hearts, keeping them as a part of their lives. Inspired by this rich tradition, we innovated a ritual where we didn't have one. We invited the children and everyone else to choose a flower from the bouquets we brought, and to share a favorite story or memory of Brian as they placed it on his grave. Most poignant were the words of his four-year-old daughter as she cradled a soft purple iris in her tiny fingers before placing it on his headstone: "I remember how Daddy gave me big hugs. And I miss him." It was one of the most powerful experiences we had as a family in the years after we lost Brian. We all listened. We all talked. Unlike that long year of grief, that day we all had something to say, and something to do. We all knew we weren't alone. And suddenly Brian did not feel so far away.

It is worth noting the sense of oneness that we felt as we participated in this ritual. This resonates with my experience at my father's graveside service, when I saw the flag draped over his casket. Rituals have therapeutic value for us partly because they are designed to make it harder for us to feel isolated. They are communal, they involve traditions that are passed on within families and within entire cultures—thus binding us together with those who have practiced them before and all who will practice them after us—as well as those who observe them in different places. Six months after losing my father, I visited the graves of my grandmother's parents, and I had a stunning realization: I was standing exactly where my grandmother had stood with her young children some eighty years earlier, grieving the loss of her parents. I imagined her standing there as a young mother, overcome with grief but finding a way to go on, and continuing to become the warm, generous woman all of her grandchildren loved. I found great solace in realizing that I was walking in the footsteps of this woman I so admired, and that we shared this experience, even though she was gone. She had endured, and so would I.

In an important way, visiting the graves of my great-grandparents that day kept my grandmother alive and present to me. In the case of funerals and remembrances of the dead, including visiting graves, rituals give us a way to remain connected to those we have lost. Rituals have therapeutic value because they provide protected spaces in which we are able to express our feelings openly with and to others, and to reflect on our lives and the lives of others. They are good for us, and that's why the ancient Confucian philosopher Xunzi compared rituals to markers that help us cross a river: "Those who cross waters mark out the deep places, but if the markers are not clear, then people will fall in. . . . The rituals are those markers."

What wisdom can Chinese philosophers offer to us in a culture that is often devoid of traditional rituals? Can we really learn from Chinese philosophers how to parent using rituals, when we aren't living in as ritualistic a culture as they were? I think the answer to this is a resounding "yes" because Chinese philosophy gives us a starting place for innovating and inventing rituals that can be meaningful and effective for us. For ancient Chinese philosophers, ritual practice was largely a matter of recovering or preserving rituals that were a part of their culture. But as we have seen, they offer a variety of ideas and suggestions that can be applied today. My family and I found that simply by thinking about Confucian views of what rituals are and what they are supposed to do for us, we were able to create a meaningful graveside ritual where we otherwise would not have had one.

Confucian philosophers urge us to think creatively about how we can make all types of occasions more meaningful and enriching through the addition of rituals. Sometimes, we must innovate them. My husband and I had long wanted to find a more meaningful way to observe Advent with our children, and when we happened upon Christmas pyramids at a Christmas village one year, we decided to build our own ritual. Every night during Advent season, we turn out the lights, light the candles on the Christmas pyramid, and as it starts to spin, together we sing the Advent song that I grew up singing in church each Sunday of Advent. It's a combination of new and old, tradition and innovation.

When I was growing up, one of my friends never did playdates on Sundays because Sunday was "family day." Her family reserved that day solely for spending time together. There were no exceptions: it was protected, sacred space devoted to family time, and to rest. Similarly, many American families traditionally have Sunday dinner as a gathering time—again, protected, sacred space that everyone observes and honors. Confucius would have loved these rituals, and would urge busy families today to consider how they can establish or revive weekly rituals that offer times of rest and quality time together as a family. Daily rituals of this sort can also be important, and rituals at children's bedtimes can not only help to cultivate virtues like gratitude, but also have a therapeutic effect: they can help kids to settle down to sleep. For some families, this may be a time for prayer or meditation, but religious and nonreligious families alike might consider adding the ritual of having each family member share at least one thing they are grateful for from the day, and something that they need help with or are worried about. Such rituals have the added benefit of encouraging open sharing of feelings and experiences within families, and when this is done every night, without fail, as a ritual, it doesn't fall through the cracks of busy schedules.

In defining rituals very broadly, we are also invited to consider how some of our everyday commitments might be invested with deeper meaning if we view them as rituals. After my father died, I told a friend that we really wanted to find ways of honoring him. He acknowledged that there are many excellent ways to do this, including donations to charities and endowments for scholarships in a person's name. But then he told me something that struck me as deeply Confucian. After his mother had died, he came to view caring for his father as a way of honoring his mother—and that had invested an experience that was often difficult with new meaning. From a Confucian standpoint, the actions we take when caring for the people we love can and should be treated as ritual acts—for what could be more worth our care, attention, and reverence? Here again we see the sacred in the everyday.

There are numerous examples of contemporary rituals that families can transform by applying Confucian insights. Like the care that farmers and gardeners provide for tender sprouts, rituals help children grow into people who are able to express love and gratitude for others in meaningful ways, while also finding meaning and fulfillment in doing so. Confucian philosophers believed that this is best done not by having elaborate, expensive celebrations. Instead, we should embrace simple practices that help our children to think more about others and their relationships to them, much like good farmers cultivate sprouts not by imposing an artificial structure on them, but by removing weeds and watering them when there isn't enough rain, and covering them when the weather turns cold, providing cultivation when and where it is needed so that what is already there can grow and thrive.

2

Sprouts in Nature and the Dao of Sticks

'Tis the gift to be simple, 'tis the gift to be free
'Tis the gift to come down where you ought to be,
And when we find ourselves in the place just right
'Twill be in the valley of love and delight . . .
'Tis a gift to be loving, 'tis a gift to be fair
'Tis a gift to wake and breathe the morning air . . .
—"SIMPLE GIFTS" (SHAKER HYMN)

Sages practice non-action and so do not ruin. . . . They study
what is not studied and return to what the multitude pass by.
—THE *Daodejing*

n 2007, the *Washington Post* conducted an experiment. In the middle of morning rush hour, internationally acclaimed violinist Joshua Bell, dressed in jeans and a T-shirt, positioned himself against a wall beside a trash can in the L'Enfant Plaza Metro Station—the nucleus of federal Washington—opened his violin case, removed his violin, swiveled the case to face pedestrian traffic, and began to play. "Each passerby had a quick choice to make, one familiar to commuters in any urban area where the occasional street performer is part of the cityscape: Do you stop and listen? Do you hurry past with a blend of guilt and irritation, aware of your cupidity but annoyed by the unbidden demand on your time and your wallet? Do you throw in a buck, just to be polite? Does your decision change if he's really bad? What if he's really good? Do you have time for beauty? Shouldn't you? What are the moral mathematics of the moment?"[1]

That morning, those questions were answered in a very public way, since the musician standing against the wall at the top of the escalators was one of the finest classical musicians in the world, playing some of the most elegant music ever written, on one of the most valuable violins ever made. Three days before, Bell had played to a sold-out crowd where reasonably good seats went for $100.

Two weeks later, he would play to a standing-room-only audience in the Washington area that was "so respectful of his artistry that they stifled their coughs until the silence between movements." But although the staff at the *Post* had discussed how to handle the possible mob scene that could result as people recognized Bell, they did not anticipate the actual turn of events that morning.

Over the course of 43 minutes, as he performed six classical pieces, 1,097 people passed by. Seven people stopped to take in the performance, at least for a minute. Twenty-seven gave money, most of them on the run—for a total of $32.17. Only one person recognized him and stood there taking in the remainder of his performance, appalled that her fellow commuters were throwing small change into his case. The other 1,070 people hurried by, oblivious, many only a few feet away, with very few of them even turning to look.

When interviewed by the *Post* a few hours later, some people explained that "they were busy, had other things on their mind." Some had earbuds in and could not hear him. Some, using cell phones, spoke louder as they passed by. Many did not remember there having been a musician in the subway at all. The *Post* noted that there was no ethnic or demographic pattern to distinguish those who stopped to watch Bell or gave money, with one very important exception: "Every single time a child walked past, he or she tried to stop and watch. And every single time, a parent scooted the kid away."

Ancient Daoist philosophers would love this story. And

it is the best story I know for showing why ancient Daoist philosophers believed that children are naturally good. *But wait*, you say. *Children are selfish! They don't share, and they cry when they don't get their way.* As a mother of three young children, I would hardly dispute the fact that they are not exactly models of benevolence. But the ancient Daoist tradition urges us to *look closer*. There are many ways in which growth and maturity changes us for the better. But there are also many ways in which it changes us for the worse. Think back to those children in the subway. Every last one of them tried to stop to listen. And every time, their grownup pulled them away.

THE GREATEST CARVING

Ancient Daoist philosophers (including the authors of the earliest Daoist texts the *Daodejing* and the *Zhuangzi*, from the third and fourth centuries BCE) believed that human beings are originally good: from birth, we already know the most important things we need to know. Unlike Confucian philosophers who thought we needed to be cultivated and refined with the help of rituals, traditions, and teachers—like little sprouts needing to be nurtured or little pieces of jade or ivory waiting to be carved into a beautiful shape—the ancient Daoists believed that the carving or cultivation meant to help us become extraordinary in fact destroys something that is already good. They likened us to ornate pieces of driftwood with a beautiful shape and colorful natural lines, worthy of being displayed and admired by all. This is why the *Daodejing* says, "The greatest carving cuts nothing off."[2] To carve such beautiful wood would be a tragedy: it would destroy the natural beauty that is already there, and which cannot possibly be improved upon through any artificial design or through the use of any artificial instrument.

What exactly did ancient Daoist philosophers see in infants and young children that they found so admirable? At first glance, we might be inclined to dismiss these claims as implausible and unrealistic. Infants and young children are certainly unrefined or "uncarved," but is this really a good thing?

Whereas the ancient Confucians believed the Dao ("the Way") was a clear path or way of living for humans that was made up of rituals, customs, virtues, and meaningful relationships, the ancient Daoists thought the Dao was more elusive. Daoists thought that Confucians were sadly mistaken in thinking they could clearly articulate and understand how to follow it because in fact "The Way that can be followed is not a constant Way; the name that can be named is not a constant name."[3] While Confucians believed the Way was something that you have to make and maintain, like a path or road that gets you through the woods, the Daoists urged us to float upon rivers and lakes, unpremeditated meandering highways through the natural world. They argued that the Confucians misunderstood the true nature of the Dao, and that it was not a path made up of human practices and virtues, but rather a dynamic entity: an impersonal force that is at once part of all of the things in the world but also beyond all things. All of us are born in harmony with the Dao. Indeed, Daoists referred to the Dao as "the mother of the myriad creatures" and "the mother of Heaven and earth" because they believed it to be the origin and life-giver of all things, but they did not see it as a deity or being.

Nevertheless, like the Confucians, they believed we should try to follow the Dao. But for the Daoists, this doesn't mean observing rituals or cultivating virtues; it means getting in touch with our originally good nature and following the perfect moral compass within ourselves. It means learning to move with the rhythms of the Dao, to bring our lives into harmony with it. And when we do this, we will be in harmony with ourselves, with other humans and animals, and with the rest of nature—we will be able to lead happy and fulfilling lives. But it is important to remember that for the Daoists, this is always a process of returning to or overcoming estrangement from the Dao, rather than discovering something that we did not know before.

What, then, goes wrong? How do we become estranged from the Dao, and why do we need to return to it? Part of the answer is that we easily become consumed with the details of our lives and forget that we are a very small part of a much larger picture. Daoist philosophers believed that we become estranged from the Dao and begin to lose our original goodness as a result of socialization. We come to believe that we need to embellish our original nature and are enticed to pursue excessive wealth, artificial standards of beauty, prestige, and power as a way of doing this. In short, we become achievement oriented, an artificial and harmful view on life. But the pursuit of artificial goals upsets the natural balance, obscuring and hindering our original nature rather than improving it. We become blinded to our true, good, and natural desires, and this leads to both physical and psychological distress.

One of the things we must do to recover our original nature and overcome our estrangement from the Dao is to recognize our true and natural place in the world. We are not separate from or more important than the rest of nature, but rather one small part of it. Daoist landscape paintings illustrate this view beautifully. From a distance, they appear to consist solely of vast landscapes including trees, lakes, waterfalls, clouds, and sky. But if you approach the painting and look very closely, you will see people tucked into the landscape, small and unimposing. In fact, the humans in Daoist landscape paintings are so small that if you do not look closely, you will miss them entirely. Ideally, the ancient Daoists believed, we will accord with nature in this way, not imposing ourselves on it or regarding our own agendas as more important, but seeing ourselves as an extension of it, and looking for ways to appreciate and be part of it. When asked what virtues we hope to see in our children, most of us would name things like honesty and generosity, but the Daoists thought that noticing and appreciating the beauty around us is especially important.

This view is appealing, but notice how it stands in tension with an achievement-oriented view. When we become estranged from the Dao through socialization, we begin to find the idea that we are small and insignificant troubling. We live in a world that encourages us to stand out and to be exceptional in order to win prestige and admiration. Many of the Daoist observations readily apply to our modern society and its values, and it is important to note that the Daoists decisively reject these values.

SIMPLE GIFTS

What is it about children that made ancient Daoist philosophers think we are originally good? They knew that at first glance, children do not appear to be good. But appearances are misleading. Daoists were fascinated by how infants and young children *appear* to be anything but admirable—when in fact they are highly admirable. For example, they pointed out that newborn infants appear to be weak, and yet are in fact quite strong in certain ways: "Those steeped in virtue are like newborn children . . . Their bones are weak and sinews yielding and yet their grip is firm . . . They can wail all day without growing hoarse."[4] The characteristics they highlight here are accurate. Newborns have an exceptionally strong-fisted grip. Every parent remembers the feeling of those tiny fingers wrapped around theirs. Also memorable: trying to unclench my newborns' fists in order to wash the palms of their hands while giving them a bath—it is no small challenge. Equally exceptional is their ability to cry loudly and persistently without growing hoarse. Parents who have had colicky infants can attest to this. Between the ages of six weeks and four months, our oldest daughter did not exactly "wail all day," but she did cry for seven hours straight, from 4 p.m. to 11 p.m. each day. She never grew hoarse. Infants also naturally know to eat when they are hungry and stop when they are full. Studies actually confirm that they will stop eating only when they have consumed the amount of fat their body needs—whether that means drinking multiple bottles with lower fat content or one bottle with higher fat content.

These are things that infants do effortlessly. They are also abilities that we lose as we grow. As adults, we must work to maintain a strong-fisted grip. We must warm up our voices in order to avoid growing hoarse, and we lose or injure our voices much more easily. Nutritionists now encourage parents of toddlers to try to help them *retain* their natural awareness of when they are hungry or full by paying attention to it, since the loss of this sensibility can be so detrimental. And Daoists would point out that eating disorders in teens and adults are typically driven by a desire to conform to an artificial standard of beauty imposed on us by society, and which leads us to resist our body's natural needs and inclinations. Although this is anecdotal, I personally have seen many young women in my classes struggle with these artificial and often impossible standards of beauty.

But original goodness is not just about physical traits. Early Daoist philosophers noticed that children relate to the world around them in a very different way, likely because they have not yet learned to embrace society's goals. There are a host of admirable qualities to notice here, including their natural curiosity and their ability to find and take joy in the everyday beauty that surrounds us. This is at least partly because they do not see themselves as separate from and superior to the rest of creation; they have a sense of oneness with it. This leads them to feel *at home* in the world in a way that few adults do. The *Daodejing* expresses these things beautifully in the following lines: "If you are a canyon for all the world, constant virtue will never leave you, and you can return home to be a child."[5] Infants and children are enviable for not yet having lost what we must work hard to regain. They are unself-conscious, displaying an ease and comfort in who and what they are that serves as a contrast to the aggressive, competitive ways of many adults and older children.

Early Daoist philosophers are not *just* saying that we don't notice how admirable children are (e.g., they appear weak but are actually strong in many ways). They are also saying that we *don't value* many of the good things about children. For instance, if asked to name the three people we most admire, few of us would include the name of an infant or a young child. Why? Because we tend to admire people who have overcome adversity or achieved great things. Infants and young children *haven't done much,* or at least they don't do things we regard as significant achievements. In the Daoist view, therein lies the problem. Many of the things we value—such as being active, autonomous, and achieving the kinds of things that might lead us to be regarded as exceptional—are in fact not the things we should value at all (or at least not as highly). The fact that children *lack* them is actually a virtue on their part.

The text of the *Zhuangzi* tells us that sages appear "vague and aimless, yet wander beyond the dirt and dust; they are free and easy, tending to nothing as their job."[6] While we see it as a drawback to be aimless and not have a job—which is one of the reasons most of us would not list young children as those we most admire—in fact this aimlessness allows children to enjoy a host of benefits that we as adults do not: they freely wander beyond the dirt and dust of the world (or, at least, they play in it), appreciating natural wonder and beauty while we pass it by without so much as a glance. On a related note, the *Daodejing* contends that "Those who preserve the Dao do not desire fullness. Because they are not full, they have no need for renewal."[7] Infants and very young children do not have agendas or desires to *achieve* certain things. They follow their every whim, spontaneous and unfettered.

One important thing we can do for our children, then, is to try to give them the extra time and space to spontaneously explore and appreciate the world around them. When I first started to take this Daoist lesson seriously and apply it to my own parenting, I quickly realized it was going to mean leaving early for things in order to build in time for my children to stop and look at spiderwebs in the bushes or listen to various birdsongs. It's not realistic to do this all of the time, but I can be intentional about doing it sometimes. I notice that I, too, am happier, when we can walk slowly together and notice the beauty around us. (And, I admit, the image of those parents who pulled their children past Josh Bell in the subway also motivates me.) Another, related thing we can do is try to ensure that our kids spend more unstructured free time in nature. Young children's spontaneity—a virtue that Daoist philosophers prized—often promotes a deeper engagement with nature. They shift their attention quickly and completely, which is an asset in nature. A child might be completely focused on one activity, such as taking a trip to the park, and then step outside and immediately become absorbed in something else—often something more remarkable, such as a butterfly—and completely forget about their previous activity. The Daoists view this as one of the marks of sages: their ability to respond spontaneously and savor the often-fleeting opportunities that come to us with each passing moment. They give their attention with ease. This is what enables them to stop and notice ladybugs and dewdrops in the grass—or Josh Bell playing in the subway—while the rest of us hurry past.

The natural tendency of children to *stop and attend* to things when adults would rush by, distracted, is one of the most important characteristics celebrated by Daoist philosophers. Ironically, we usually see our children as too easily distracted when they do this. Ancient Daoist philosophers focused on a certain type of inactivity—which they called *wuwei* (無為)—"effortless action"—as one of our original abilities. While *wuwei* is sometimes misunderstood as suggesting that we should do nothing, the *Daodejing* insists that we should "Act, but through *wuwei*."[8] *Wuwei* actions are effortless, natural, and never forceful or aggressive; they also promote our well-being and help us to flourish. As the Asian studies professor Edward Slingerland puts it, the experience of *wuwei* is "relaxing and enjoyable, but in a deeply rewarding way" that distinguishes it from many other experiences.[9]

Young children act in a *wuwei* fashion when they stop and attend to the everyday beauty around them; Daoists see this as an ability that enables us to lead a flourishing life. Children do it easily, but we lose this ability over time as we are pulled into the busy world around us. Ancient Daoist texts highlight this ability in children and connect it to the Dao: "I alone am still and inactive . . . like a child who has not yet learned to smile. . . . Weak and weary, I seem to have nowhere to go."[10]

There are many examples of how this ability to *stop* and *attend* distinguishes young children from the rest of us. Very young children do not tear open all of their gifts at a fast pace on Christmas morning. Often unaware that there are other gifts waiting, they are more inclined to stop and play with each thing—and even get absorbed in playing with the packaging materials more than the gift itself, having not yet been programmed to think that the gift inside the box is of greater value. In contrast, their parents anxiously watch, eager for their child to open the next gift so they can see their reaction, while older children, who know the social custom of giving and receiving multiple gifts at Christmas, open their gifts as quickly as possible. Indeed, their parents may tell them to *slow down*! Younger children, however, often require encouragement to move on to the next package.

Ancient Daoists would argue that such examples show that gluttony and materialism—seen in the urgency to rush on to the next best thing—are not qualities that we naturally or initially exhibit, prior to the influences of socialization. Here we see why Daoists tend to regard socialization not as a natural process but an artificial one that can and should be reversed, at least to a certain degree.

Like the old Shaker hymn "Simple Gifts," ancient Daoist philosophers extol the simple gifts in life, and a simple way of being in the world. If we watch them carefully, we will see that children do seem to understand that it is, indeed, "a gift to wake and breathe the morning air."

THE MUNDANE

When my son was six years old, he came home with a Thanksgiving turkey that made me feel prouder than anything he had ever brought home before. But it wasn't the extraordinary aesthetic quality of his artwork that made me feel proud. It was what he had written on six colored feathers he had crudely cut out and glued onto his turkey—the things he was most thankful for: "spruce," "sticks," "house," "toys," "books," "family." Why did I feel proud? My son was expressing not only genuine love but also gratitude for nature by naming and highlighting specific parts of nature—the spruce tree he loved to play beside and the sticks he loved to play with—right alongside his home and family. I loved that spruce trees and sticks belonged together with home and family for him. I loved that he highlighted two different things from nature but grouped his toys together as one. I also loved that the things he chose from nature were not the flashier items adults would tend to note, like sunsets, butterflies, or autumn leaves, but things we adults tend to call *mundane*: spruce trees and sticks.

Even though I grew up in south-central Alaska, playing in the woods and on the beaches of the small fishing town where my family lived, it was the ancient Daoist texts that I spent years immersing myself in that led me to reflect on what it means to have a genuine love for nature and all of the good that it brings. Like many people, I loved nature as a child. But the ancient Daoist tradition helped me to understand why that love for nature comes so easily to young children, why it is so important to sustain and nurture that love, and how we might go about doing that for our children and for ourselves. In his book *Last Child in the Woods: Saving Our Children from Nature-Deficit Disorder*, Richard Louv shows how essential direct exposure to nature is for healthy childhood development, and how detrimental the *lack* of nature in children's lives today is—due in large part to the growth of technology.¹¹ The early Daoists, too, were concerned about the impact of technology in their own time (though it looked quite different from ours, of course) partly because they thought it would lead us to live in ways that were not as close to nature, and therefore not as good for us.

Ancient Daoist philosophers would also endorse Louv's description of the human costs of alienation from nature as a real *disorder*. They believed that when we watch young children in nature, we can see several aspects of their original goodness. They are highly observant, noticing and attending to even the smallest things, from anthills to buds on trees. They are natural explorers, examining the textures, smells, and sounds of the things they see: the rough texture of bark, the smell of the air following a rainstorm, the various birdsongs. Their natural sense of wonder and awe enables them to appreciate how extraordinary the things they encounter are.

This should lead us, in turn, to notice certain things about ourselves. We tend to be highly distracted; we often don't notice the things children notice because we literally *aren't looking* at nature. Why? It is partly because we feel pressure to get other things done, and partly because we don't expect to see anything very interesting. We also usually don't touch, smell, or examine (or taste!) the things we find in nature, partly because (at risk of sounding repetitive) *we aren't looking*, but also partly because we think we have experienced it all before. We also feel a little silly doing these things, and we do not appreciate just how extraordinary the things we see are. As we grow, we've also learned to classify things as "interesting" or "mundane." As a result of seeing many, if not most, parts of nature as mundane, we tend not to take joy in the simplest things, as children do. A sunset might take my breath away, but not the spruce tree beside our house. And yet that same spruce tree topped my son's list of things for which he was most thankful.

There is an interesting question for us to consider as parents here: Are these differences just an expression of the fact that we are more sophisticated than our children, or are we missing something important? Is our more "sophisticated" view really superior—a mark of our refinement, our ability to judge beauty in a more discerning way? Or are our children in fact more able than we are to see and discern beauty in the world around us? Depending upon how you answer these questions, further questions follow. Is it *better* to appreciate the flashier, more unusual parts of nature and pass by the everyday? Are some parts of nature *really* mundane?

The word "mundane" means "lacking interest or excitement; dull." But it also means "of this earthly world rather than a heavenly or spiritual one." Note the tendency to devalue "this earthly world" by comparison with anything else that might be out there. Whereas such a dichotomy comes easily to cultures influenced by Christianity, ancient Daoist philosophers believed that the Dao breathes life into and pulses through the natural world—even though it is also beyond it. This world is just as sacred as what lies beyond it.

Part of what leads us to call something mundane is the fact that we see it all the time. And yet note the hidden assumption here: we ought to more highly value things that are rare, compared with things we find every day. But why should I value a colorful sunset more highly than the spruce tree in my yard? On one view, I have gained sophistication through my ability to recognize a rare thing, but on another, I have lost the ability to appreciate the beauty that is around me each day. Are we more sophisticated than our children, having gained perspective on the mundane versus the extraordinary, or have we in fact lost something important that we once had—namely, the ability to recognize the value and beauty in the everyday, in all parts of nature, both simple and complex?

I believe most of us feel a measure of wonder when we watch our children take joy in the everyday parts of nature. I also think we tend to feel at least a twinge of regret and gratitude when they notice something beautiful, appealing, or fascinating that we wouldn't have seen if we hadn't been with them. Ancient Daoist philosophers would not want us to stop appreciating rare instances of beauty such as exceptional sunsets, but they would want us to stop overlooking the beauty in the everyday. They would also have us actively join our children in feeling the joy of stomping in puddles and touching dewdrops with our fingertips. And they would want us to stop labeling certain things as mundane, for in their view, this only signals something that is wrong with us—namely, that we are unable to appreciate the simple gifts and simple beauty in the world around us. Mundaneness is not an objective feature of the world, but something we impose upon it.

LOVING NATURE

In James Taylor's well-known song "Copperline," he commemorates his childhood home in North Carolina, where he spent his early years exploring nature with his dog, Hercules. Asked once about the song, Taylor remarked that it tells about "a childhood that was very peaceful, which is a rare thing today. I felt like I was part of a landscape in those days—the trees, the streams and the rivers, the animals that lived there."[12] Taylor's words here resonate with the view that we find in Daoist landscape paintings and ancient Daoist texts. And the lines at the top of the chorus—"Half a mile down to Morgan Creek; I'm only livin' 'til the end of the week"—highlight an important feature of how children encounter nature: they are *in the moment*. When they stop and squat down next to an anthill or follow a butterfly, they are not thinking about the future (or trying to capture it on their smartphone and share it with the world). And this heightens the quality of their engagement with nature, as well as their enjoyment of it.

The final verses of "Copperline" describe the devastation inflicted on the land where he grew up, including the construction of the prefabricated homes that now pepper the landscape: "I tried to go back, as if I could. All spec houses and plywood." Also a part of the picture of lost nature is the fact that *you can't go back*. We have one opportunity to live out the years of our childhood. We also have one opportunity to raise our children.

Indeed, there are further and higher stakes involved here, for we live in a world that does not value nature as it should. Although most of us want our children to have clean air to breathe and clean, healthy rivers, woodlands, and mountains to enjoy, early Daoist philosophers would point out that we often fail to see the connection between how we see nature (or fail to see it) and our care for the environment. Our views on these matters, as with others, will be transmitted to our children as they grow. This is seen in a variety of different areas. As children grow, we tend to encourage them to *do* something when they are outside: to play soccer or baseball, and ride bikes—all wonderful activities, but sometimes, they replace the time in nature that young children are more often accorded. If we do give our older children time in nature, we might be inclined to give them some type of assignment, perhaps encouraging them to research the things they see.

It is important to ask ourselves *why* we tend to encourage older children to do these things. For one, we are encouraging them to build skills and abilities in certain areas and to do things that are edifying. We are also encouraging them to get exercise, and preventing them from getting bored, having too much screen time, or getting into trouble. Indeed, older children may also be interested in doing other things; they may find it uninteresting to be outdoors if they do not have someone or something to play with, such as a bicycle, scooter, or soccer ball.

Not all of these things are negative. But ancient Daoist philosophers would encourage us to consider carefully the distinctive goods associated with how younger children encounter nature, and to see how we might preserve these goods as our children grow instead of simply seeing them as an inevitable loss—and a loss that is natural and good as we grow and develop into more sophisticated beings! We do not have to choose between having our children play team sports and having our children truly love nature and become committed to caring for it, but we do have to attend carefully to our children's schedules in order to intentionally make room for free time spent in nature. This does not always have to be isolated time, nor does it have to be wholly noninstructional or inactive. Spending time in nature with our children creates a regular opportunity for an ongoing dialogue about the world, our place within it, and how things live and grow. And it is an opportunity to learn *with* our children about a wide range of plants, animals, and other parts of the natural world.

Consider the example of the celebrated entomologist and conservationist E. O. Wilson. His love of ants began as a child, not just as an intellectual curiosity but as a genuine *passion* for insects. Had he not had the opportunity to spend time absorbed in nature, he would never have followed the path he did. He went on to become not only one of the world's leading biologists, but also a passionate environmental activist. His concern for the future of our planet and his renowned work as a scientist grew out of a love of nature that began in his childhood.

Most parents today want their children to develop a commitment to caring for the environment, and the Daoist tradition offers a variety of insights into how we can best achieve this goal. To begin, early Daoist philosophers would argue that a desire to care for nature is something to be preserved and nurtured in children—for we are not teaching them to love nature, but allowing their natural love of nature to develop fully. Daoist philosophers would also emphasize that if we want our children to live a life that involves caring for the environment, they must not only *understand* the impact of such things as climate change and pollution, but they must also have certain *feelings* about nature, and genuinely care about and love it. Giving children the gift of time to spend in nature has irreplaceable importance in nurturing these things. But we must take care to ensure *quality* time in nature as our children grow—time that is not spent trying to score goals on a soccer field, but simply attending to, enjoying, playing in, and engaging with nature in a hands-on way. Such experiences nurture a love of nature and motivate us to do more to protect, preserve, and restore our environment. And the early Daoists believed that this was good both for our children—and for nature, too.

Early Daoist philosophers would also remind us that our children have as much (or more) to teach us as we have to teach them. They would also caution us against making our time in nature *overly* instructional or athletic. It is difficult to notice and savor the natural world when you are constantly learning life cycles or completing a challenging hike—although these might be complementary activities if time is allotted for both. We might label activities like observing and savoring the beauty of songbirds as "passive" activities, and many would value them less highly than "more active" pursuits with clear goals or outcomes that might bring tangible rewards. The early Daoists would label them *wuwei* activities, and value them more highly because they bring the most important rewards: the intangible ones. In those Daoist landscape paintings, there is always plenty of empty space to remind us of the importance of it in our own lives.

Many of the good things that our children can teach us are, after all, harder than memorizing information or honing athletic ability: how to stop and observe, notice, and attend to even the smallest, most ordinary things; how to explore those things using all of our senses and remain in the moment feeling wonder, awe, and gratitude for the extraordinary world in which we live; and how to genuinely love and take joy in nature—all of its parts, from sticks and spruce trees to extraordinary sunsets. These lessons, though learned in nature, can be extended to the rest of our lives and our children's lives. Learning to stop, attend closely, listen, and be in the moment, experiencing all of the wonder and joy that life has to offer, represents an attitude toward life that would serve us well in any situation we might encounter.

Nature also opens up a unique opportunity for children

to use and grow their imaginations. While there are many skills that can be learned through structured activities, there are few places that are better than outside in nature for allowing a child's imagination and creativity to thrive on its own and develop naturally. Playing in nature, children are not limited by toys; they can—and must—use their imagination to create any world they choose from the things and spaces they find. Free play in nature in a sense resembles a blank piece of paper for a child to draw on. Coloring books help children to build important skills, but blank paper allows a child's imagination and creativity to be wholly unbounded. Creative, imaginative space—in other words, empty and unscheduled time—is another area that we tend to fill up too quickly for our children, often because it doesn't seem to *yield results* in the same way that playing team sports or working math problems does.

Here we see that early Daoist philosophers are urging us to take things other than academic or athletic achievement as our primary goals. In their view, the best kind of life is not measured by these types of achievements or by such things as how prestigious your job is or how much money you make. Some of the basic features of a good life are the very things that young children do so easily in nature: they observe, attend to, explore, savor, stand in awe of, appreciate, love, and take joy in the world around them. This way of being in the world—in relation not only to other people but also to other animals, plants, and other living and nonliving things—is one of the keys to leading a happy, satisfying, and flourishing life.

⚜ 3 ⚜

Watching Sprouts Grow:
The Dao of Mindfulness

One must, at all times, be like a cat catching mice—with eyes intently watching and ears intently listening.

—WANG YANGMING

Human beings can broaden the Way—it is not the Way that broadens human beings.

—CONFUCIUS

When I was a child, my best friend Sabrina lived at the top of a gravel road that ran parallel to my road, both on a downhill slope stretching toward the beach. Sabrina's house was at the top of the hill; mine was at the bottom, but our roads were connected by a well-worn path through the forest that opened up behind my house. In order to get to Sabrina's house for our regular playdates, I would walk the forest path and then up Sabrina's road. When it was time to go home, however, I was always hesitant. "It's such a long way!" I would tell her, frowning. "I have to walk all the way down your road and then all the way through the forest to get home." Gazing at me sympathetically, Sabrina would say, "You're right! I'll walk you halfway!" And off we would go, down the road. But when we reached the opening of the forest path, and Sabrina would say she had to head home, I would inevitably say, "Wait, but I still have to go all the way through the forest, and it's dark in there!" And Sabrina would reply, "You're right! Let me walk you halfway through the woods." And we would set out on the mossy path covered with rust-colored spruce needles, winding between birch trees and spruce trees, watermelon berry plants and fiddlehead ferns. About halfway through the forest, Sabrina stopped. "Wait. Now I have to go back through the forest and up my road! That's farther than you have to go." And I would say, "You're right! I'll walk you halfway back." And back we would go, until the forest path ended and we found ourselves once more walking along Sabrina's road toward her house. Again I stopped, saying, "Wait! But now I have to go back through the forest again. Will you go partway with me?" And so it went on. Once, my mom called Sabrina's mother to find out where I was, and Sabrina's mother looked out her window, saying "She's on the way—I see them heading down the road, almost to the woods. Oh, no, wait. Now they're headed back this way!"

One of the traditional Confucian images of the Dao (the Way) is a well-worn path stretching through a forest. Confucian philosophers understood the Dao as a human-made path or way of life that is made up of all of our patterns of living, our social customs, our rituals, values, ideals, and the virtues we cultivate. Confucius refers to "the virtues that constitute the Way of the cultivated person," making clear that it isn't just *any* path, but the path one follows when leading a good life.[1] It has been worn and preserved by all who have walked this path before us, including our grandparents and parents, others we admire and who have contributed to the way of life that we strive to follow. It is also the path that Confucius dedicates his life to teaching about, which is why he says, "Having in the morning heard that the Way was being put into practice, I could die that evening without regret."[2] Indeed, the

Way is dynamic—something that we practice and follow actively in all of the things, large and small, that make up living a good life.

Relationships are always paramount for Confucians. Thus, the Dao is ultimately created through human relationships, which is what makes the forest path worn by Sabrina and me so apt. It is through our shared life that the Dao was created and is maintained. But it is not entirely fixed, and neither was the path that Sabrina and I walked. Each summer, the path would look a little different due to changes in the world around us—tree roots that grew out into the path and threatened to trip us, or tree limbs that had snapped under the weight of the winter snow. We would then adjust the path slightly—widening it or moving it to the right or left to avoid obstacles. Sabrina and I learned the importance of these adjustments the hard way. As we walked, we loved looking up at the songbirds flitting through the trees, and the patches of sky seeping through the outstretched limbs of the trees. One year, on one of the first spring forays through the woods, while gazing upward at the trees, I tripped on a fallen tree branch that blocked the path, and badly bloodied my knee. It was painful, and I had to limp home instead of going to Sabrina's. From then on, we were meticulous about the path. We wanted it to be clear of hazards so that we could enjoy our walks in the woods. This meant we had to broaden it and move it, adjusting the path year to year. But the path didn't change much. It remained the same path, just with slightly different bends at certain points.

TECHNOLOGY AND THE DAO OF PARENTING

Our forest path offers a beautiful illustration of the Dao. It is a clear path for us to follow and has a consistent core, and yet it is dynamic due to the inevitable changes in our lives. Confucius says, "Human beings can broaden the Way—it is not the Way that broadens human beings," and indeed, Sabrina and I broadened our path in various ways from year to year, altering it as we walked along in order to avoid obstacles and pitfalls.[3] The sense of the term for "broaden" in classical Chinese here also means to "extend" or "fill out." The path was worn through our friendship— day in, day out, traveling that path together or alone to play together. And so, too, do we wear patterns of life through the things we do with our families and friends. We practice traditions and rituals, we work to cultivate virtues and values in ourselves and our children, and we find meaning in relationships with friends and family. We walk a well-worn path, and we maintain that path through our own footsteps.

And yet, for as much continuity as there is—my desire for my children to be kind, grateful, and resilient is the same as that of my parents and grandparents—there are also differences from generation to generation. The path changes in places—it requires active and intentional broadening on our part, often in order to deal with obstacles. One of the most striking areas of cultural change that creates this necessity is technology. I often tell my students that although much of what is required in order to be a good student is the same for them as it was for me when I was in college, there are also some ways in which the Dao has been—or has to be—broadened for them as a result of new forms of technology. When I started college, email was not widely used, and the advent of social media and smartphones had not yet begun. These new forms of technology have changed our lives in the years since. Today, my students must find ways of dealing with the constant distractions of social media and texting—distractions that I did not encounter as a student. To be sure, I *did* encounter distractions. While the distractions differ today, being a good student remains the same: virtues such as inquisitiveness, perseverance, creativity, and the ability to focus single-mindedly still represent the core of the Dao in this part of life. I do think, however, that in some ways today's distractions loom larger and are harder to avoid.

The same is true in parenting, of course. When I was growing up, my parents did not have smartphones, and so were never tempted to check their email or text a friend while they were pushing me on the swings. We talked, often, and about many things. They gave me their undivided attention. It is not that they did not have a choice in this—they absolutely did, and I realize that they made sacrifices in order to do so. They could have chosen to do other things; many parents did. But due to information technology and its prevalence in the culture, it is more tempting—and therefore more common—for parents today to divide their attention between their children and something else. Children are also more likely to find their parents interrupted by texts that seem to demand constant replies. Now, notice here that roughly the same virtues constitute the Dao of parenting for us today as for our parents and grandparents: patience, generosity, love, kindness, creativity . . . and yet we might be more tempted than previous generations to add attentiveness or mindfulness to that list. It is rarer, and more difficult to achieve.

I have seen parents bring their smartphones out on the dance floor with them in parent-toddler dance classes and use them—and not just to take pictures of their toddlers. It is a widespread practice for parents waiting at soccer practice, swim classes, martial arts classes, and "watching" their children at playgrounds to use their smartphones almost the entire time. And of course, sometimes we have good reasons for doing this. More than ever before, American parents today are juggling careers as well as caring for families. A variety of studies have shown that fathers are more involved with their children than previous generations and thus doing more juggling of their careers and childcare. Studies have also shown that working mothers still carry the lion's share of domestic labor, including childcare. Parents feel pulled in multiple directions much of the time. But what other layers are a part of our story when it comes to technology and parenting? Is our use of smartphones when we are with our children completely harmless—to our children and to ourselves? Better yet, when we are constantly on our phones at our kids' practices, classes, and at the playground, are we missing opportunities that might result in richer relationships with our children and with each other? And do we find here an opportunity to *broaden the Dao* in the way that Confucius described—to move, widen, or extend the path that we walk as parents so that it goes around a significant obstacle that might cause us pain or undermine our flourishing—preventing us from finding joy in life as much as we might? The day that I bloodied my knee while walking our forest path serves as an interesting illustration for us to consider.

One of the most fascinating things about Chinese philosophers is that they have as much to say to us about *how to be with* our children as they do about *what to do* with our children. Confucian and Daoist philosophers urge us to pay attention and reflect carefully on what we are doing and why. They tell us to be mindful and attentive in the things that we do as parents. If we take this seriously, we must reflect on what distracts us, and for most parents today, technology represents the primary thing that prevents us from giving our children undivided attention. Of course, it is not that we should give our children our undivided attention all of the time; it is good for children to play on their own or with friends, without parental intervention. (I do grant that sometimes, our use of technology is not an obstacle to our children's flourishing or to our flourishing.) But that is precisely why this area of our lives calls for more reflection: it is not as simple as saying that we should never use our phones when we are with our children.

Here, the Confucian tradition serves as an interesting resource, for it emphasized two things right from the start: (1) we must reflect on what we are doing and why, and form intentional habits so that they align with our values and goals in life; and (2) being parents ought to make us better people. Parenthood represents a special opportunity for self-cultivation. For although we are no longer fragile sprouts like our children, mature plants, too, can wither or bend when they aren't getting enough of what they need. Accordingly, one thing that Confucian philosophers would be keen to point out here is that our use of technology ought not to be something that just enriches—or undermines—our children's flourishing; it also represents an area that can contribute to—or undermine—our own flourishing.

This point is underscored by successful early childhood intervention programs that work with high-risk families, including many parents who never had positive models in their own parents. One of the many things that staff in these programs teach parents are skills to encourage parents to *play with their children*, helping them to see that if they do, they will enjoy being with their children more. Fundamentally, this is a lesson about attention and how it contributes to our overall happiness as well as the well-being of our children. And while playing with your children is something that virtually all readers of this book know the importance of, how well do we do it? The words of the *Daodejing* are apropos here: "These are things everyone in the world knows but none can practice." It might be helpful to extend the basic lesson here to all parents: if you give your child your undivided attention when you are at the playground together, you will enjoy it a lot more, and your child will, too. Of course, when we have fun with our children, we are building—and maintaining—a relationship with them. After all, Confucian philosophers will note that relationship is what everything hinges on. They argue that the relationship between parents and children serves as the foundation of a child's entire development— it is, as they put it, the "root" from which a child's character grows—and they believe the quality of the relationship you have with your child holds the key here.[4] Confucians are keen to point out that the kind of loving, supportive relationships that children thrive on cannot be nurtured without really *being with* them—that is, being *fully present* with them, in the sense that Confucius meant when he talked about being fully present at rituals—for that is the way that any relationship is built and sustained.

Early Confucian philosophers also understood that the relationship between parent and child begins when the child is a newborn—something that has been clearly established by modern scientific research. They did not dismiss infants and toddlers but believed—long before anything like modern science existed to confirm it—that the earliest stages of children's development are absolutely critical. This is why they wrote about how the ancient sages were cared for attentively even from the time they were infants who were still being swaddled. Caregivers who assisted families in raising these young sages from the time they were infants and toddlers were selected for their moral virtues because Confucians understood that our character is formed deeply by those who care for us, right from the start. Early Confucian philosophers even argued for the importance of good prenatal care for children's future development. They understood that the task of parenting—of making sacrifices for your child and thereby shaping the sort of person she will become—begins before birth.

Most of us can see the importance of giving our children our attention when we are interacting with them. But is it the same when we are watching our children during soccer or swim practice? For some, watching soccer practice is mind-numbingly boring. In response, both Confucian and Daoist philosophers would be inclined to ask us if we are *really watching*. Both of these traditions stress mindfulness—attending to the small details of our lives, moment to moment, day to day. "Being mindful" sounds appealing to everyone, but in parenting, giving your children your undivided attention can be a tall order. It means looking into their eyes, watching them learn to swim, watching them play beside their favorite tree or at the park, and it means pointing out the beauty in nature and in the lives of those around them. It also means noticing that our children are watching us more closely than we usually realize. It is easy to miss that if you aren't watching *them* carefully, but if you are, you will see their heads turn, and their eyes light up when they see that you *see* them. While technology can be a great asset in teaching our children and helping them to keep in touch with family and friends, it often prevents us from being mindful of our children—even if we are looking at mindfulness apps!

Mindfulness has indeed become popular, largely due to the popularity of secularized forms of Buddhist meditation. In all of these traditions, mindfulness is about learning to pay attention to, appreciate, and reflect on things that we could easily miss, but ancient Confucian and Daoist philosophers valued mindfulness for some different reasons than Buddhists do. The main goal, for Confucians, was not to attain enlightenment but to live life in a meaningful and fulfilling way—and the primary way of doing this is to have meaningful relationships. For early Daoists, too, the main goal was to live well in this life: from a Daoist perspective, we are mindful when we stop filling all of our time with ceaseless activities and embrace stillness and silence, allowing time for rest, for listening and watching and savoring the many good things that are a part of our lives.

MINDFULNESS AND ATTENTIVENESS IN PARENTING

For early Confucian philosophers, mindfulness always centers on cultivating relationships—and not just any relationships, but good relationships that make us better and make those around us better, and that lead not just to satisfaction or happiness, but joy. The Confucian Mencius maintained that all children are born with sprouts of virtue—the beginnings of goodness to be nurtured by us as parents. This is a daunting task, since moral tendencies, like sprouts, require a lot in order to flourish. But according to Mencius, "If one delights in them then they grow. If they grow then how can they be stopped? If they cannot be stopped, then without realizing it one's feet begin to step in time to them and one's hands dance according to their rhythms."[5] One of the points Mencius is making here is that we ought to *delight* in the activity of moral cultivation—finding joy in the task of nurturing our children's potential, and not just seeing it as obligatory drudgery. That act of taking joy in our children *itself* helps to nourish them, because our children see it on our faces and hear it in our voices.

Indeed, Confucius taught that people should not just follow the Way, but delight in it, even though following it can be exhausting and challenging.[6] (As he famously put it, "The burden is heavy and the Way is long."[7]) But in his view, this makes it all the more important to find ways of allowing ourselves to find joy in following the Way: "One who knows it is not the equal of one who loves it, and one who loves it is not the equal of one who takes joy in it."[8] From the standpoint of parenting, there is a key point here: it is not just that we should do right by our children as parents; we should also *enjoy* doing so, in just the same way that Sabrina and I loved following our forest path each year, savoring the nature that surrounded us as well as the joys of friendship.

Parent-child relationships have always been of special interest to Confucians when it comes to mindfulness.

Being mindful of the age of our parents, for instance, can lead us to be more grateful for and appreciative of the time we have with them and to be more aware of their changing needs. Confucius urges us to be mindful and attentive to age, for example: "You must always be aware of the age of your parents. On the one hand, it is a cause for rejoicing, on the other a source of anxiety."[9]

The same could be said of one's children's ages. This is one reason why Confucian philosophers believe that intergenerational relationships are good for us. For parents, in addition to having friends with children the same age as one's own children, it is enriching to have friends from different generations. For one thing, they offer perspective. Older parents often express to younger parents how quickly the years of children's lives pass by, urging them to enjoy and savor these years. At times, older parents are also able to see the beauty in the chaotic activities of young children (while those children's parents see only the chaos and mess)—and the fleeting nature of the years when children can act on their whims so easily. This was especially poignant for me one day when I told an older colleague (whose children are grown) a story about our three children collectively emptying and spreading the entire contents of their piggy banks until the bedroom floor was carpeted in coins. I was about to complain about how long it took to clean up, but then he closed his eyes, smiled broadly, and uttered one word: "Marvelous!" In that moment, I had a much-needed change of perspective, and we both enjoyed a laugh. Granted, it can sometimes be difficult to appreciate older parents' advice to savor the early years when you are trying to wrangle a squirming toddler at the grocery store, but in truth there is much wisdom in the observation that children grow and develop quickly. While it may seem monotonous watching your child's swim lessons week after week, you will never again have the opportunity to watch her learn to swim. And one day, you will probably wish you could. It might seem like a big time commitment in the moment, but in the grander scheme of things, it is a miniscule amount of time—but one ripe with the opportunity to *live in the moment*.

The reality of change is one of the reasons why, from a Daoist perspective, we ought to stop and be mindful of the moments before us. They pass by constantly, one after another. In the words of the early Daoist philosopher Zhuangzi, "their change is the process of destiny," and so, he writes, we ought to embrace the reality of that change by welcoming and savoring each moment as if it were the coming of spring: "Day and night, without a break, make it springtime with things. As you greet each new circumstance, generate the season in your own mind."[10] As Zhuangzi points out, stillness is a key part of this: "The sage is calm, but not because he declares calmness good. . . . When water is calm, you can see the wispy hair on your temples in it. Its surface is level and sets the standard for great builders. If water is so clear when calm, how much more so the spirit!"[11] From a Daoist perspective, being still, calm, and centered is necessary for us to be mindful and to have a clear-eyed view of our children, ourselves, and the world around us. When technology is constantly vying for our attention, we simply cannot attend in the way that is needed to see clearly.

Like Daoist philosophers, Confucians also understand the importance of stillness and single-mindedness. In addition to their belief that being mindful and attentive holds the key to cultivating meaningful relationships with others, Confucian philosophers are also deeply interested in how mindfulness enables us to cultivate ourselves and our children. Only by being attentive can we work on becoming better people and help our children to grow into better people by paying attention to our actions and to our feelings, thoughts, desires, and motivations. The later Confucian philosopher Wang Yangming wrote strikingly about the attentiveness that this process requires: "One must, at all times, be like a cat catching mice—with eyes intently watching and ears intently listening." (This quotation always reminds me of the day I was walking in the woods and spied our cat in the midst of a hunt. Instead of acting like my cuddly cat who lounged in patches of sunlight on the living room floor, when I called to him, he looked at me in alarm as if he had never seen me before in his life before resuming his activities, looking completely wild: ears pricked upward, eyes wide, tracking the birds and squirrels before him, ready to pounce at any moment.)

In parenting, this kind of attentiveness begins simply by taking the time to observe our children closely—with our "eyes intently watching and ears intently listening." The most famous parenting story in the Confucian tradition is a story about just how much a parent's attentiveness can transform a child's life. It is also the first known story of a single mother in human history: it celebrates the mother of Mencius, who gave us that brilliant metaphor of sprouts and who is also the most influential Confucian thinker after Confucius himself. Mencius's father died when he was very young, leaving his mother to raise him alone. She is the very embodiment of Confucian mindfulness. The story tells of how she watched Mencius at play, day after day, her attention focused on what he was doing. At first, they lived next to a cemetery. Like all children, Mencius imitated the things he observed and incorporated them into his play, and he was soon imitating the workers in the cemetery. Troubled by this, she began looking for a new place to live. She found a home by a marketplace, and she and Mencius settled in. Soon, though, she noticed that he was imitating the salesmen hawking goods in the marketplace—again, an unappealing prospect for her son. Again she searched for a new place to live. Finally, she found a home next to a school, and when Mencius began to imitate the teachers, she knew she had found a place they could stay.

This story is known and referenced by people throughout East Asia with the common saying, "Mencius's mother moved three times" (Chinese: 孟母三遷), widely used to remind people of the sacrifices that parenting requires, and the lengths we should be willing to go to for our kids. But it also serves to remind us of the importance of mindfulness in parenting—of being willing to take the time to really watch and listen to our children. Had Mencius's mother busied herself with other things each day when he was out playing, she might not have seen his actions, prompting her to move. (And from the standpoint of the Confucian tradition, he never would have become a great Confucian teacher.)

MINDFULNESS, RELATIONSHIPS, AND STILLNESS

In addition to helping us to meet the needs of our children, Confucian philosophers also offer us some additional reasons to put our phones away, including conversation and friendship. When we are absorbed in our phones, we don't talk to each other. Remember that the Dao is created by treading that path together; doing so creates and sustains relationships. Now, on the one hand, modern technology offers us great opportunities to connect with and remain connected to one another. A friend of ours has her daughter Facetime with her mother each afternoon after school while she fixes dinner, which is a truly wonderful example of how technology can help to build and sustain relationships while also helping parents with practical tasks such as what to do with your children while you perform basic household tasks like cooking dinner. On the other hand, when it comes to how technology impacts us onscene, when we are actually with our children and other parents at dance class, soccer practice, or the playground, there is a strong tendency for technology to undermine relationships simply because we often choose our device over the alternative. This means that parents are having fewer conversations with each other while they sit side by side than ever before, which represents missed opportunities for both parents and children to form friendships and offer one another support. The importance of all of this should not be underestimated, for parenting is such a remarkably challenging endeavor, right from the start. You can easily feel like the only parent who is struggling with something—or whose child is struggling with something (and don't *we* struggle when our children struggle?). This is an isolating experience, contributing, for some, to anxiety and depression. For some who have lived in the same place for many years and already have established friendships and perhaps family nearby, it may not seem as important to form new friendships. But Confucian philosophers would make a key point here: we ought not simply to be on the lookout for friends, but for opportunities to *be* a friend. For those who have recently moved to a new place—be it a new city, state, or just a new neighborhood, it is very important to form new friendships. And, of course, can't we all benefit from new friendships? At one time, all friendships were new. You might also wonder about the transitory nature of relationships with these other parents you sit alongside, but Daoist philosophers were keen to remind us of our discomfort with change. Our friendships with each other may only be for a short season of our lives—perhaps only one soccer season—but that doesn't mean they're not worthwhile or good for us.

(The Buddhist tradition is known for pointing out that our expectation of permanence leads us to suffer, when in fact everything in our lives is bound to change, including our social circles. Parenting offers an opportunity to stretch your comfort level with constant change, because your children and therefore your relationships are always growing and changing.)

I suspect it is not really a strong resistance to new friendships that prevents most parents from putting down their phones and striking up a conversation. Not having a felt need for (or time to spend with) more friends may contribute to the habitual use of smartphones, but there are some other key factors in play. One of those is that parents are exhausted; sometimes it is hard to muster the energy for social interaction, and burying yourself in your phone is a way of getting time to yourself while also avoiding others. Here there is an opportunity to reflect on your choices as a parent: Are you sitting through too many practices and classes? Are your children overenrolled in activities? For kids, most activities represent an alternative to screens (which compete fiercely with reading, playing games, and climbing trees), and sometimes parents schedule them partly in order to avoid too much screen time. The right number of activities should be discerned carefully by each family, depending on everyone's needs. But parents must balance their own good with their children's good (meaning that it is sometimes the right choice for a child not to do something because their parents do not feel up to driving to another activity). And your own good is bound up with your children's good. When you choose to limit activities or involvements because it is too much for you, it is likely that your children would find it to be too much as well. But even if they wouldn't, a part of what children learn through their relationships in a family, including their parents, is that the world does not revolve solely around them: let's seek the good of others, and make sacrifices for the well-being of those we love.

Another related reason for the heavy smartphone use is that parents always feel that they have something to do, and increasingly, many of those things can be done on our phones. But more than any of these, I suspect that there is simply an uncritical habit of using smartphones as "down time," and this is a habit that spreads due to our social nature (but which is not, ultimately, pro-social). Without thinking, we conform because everyone else is doing it. And that's not a good reason. This idea of smartphone use as down time is very interesting to me. Confucian and Daoist philosophers would be keen to convince us that we are making a mistake when we see it as "down time," and that instead, we should work to see these times as opportunities to take joy in, and learn from and about, our children.

Ancient Daoist philosophers warned us against the use of technology (remember, however, that technology meant something different to them than it does to us), and while most of us would not accept their complete dismissal of technology, we can nevertheless learn from their warnings. One thing that concerned them was the mistaking of technology for real times of rest. And so the *Daodejing* urges, "Make sure that even though there are labor-saving tools, they are never used."[12] In ancient China, "labor-saving tools" or different forms of technology allowed people to tend their fields more quickly, but they took away from some of the traditional ways of planting and harvesting, as well as the communal experiences that defined those ways. They allowed people to travel more easily, but this led families to spend more time apart. None of these things were considered good for people's overall flourishing, and that is why the early Daoists warned us about the use of technology. Phones are certainly labor-saving tools for us today, but what do we miss out on when we are using them instead of visiting with other parents, watching our children, or giving them our undivided attention?

As we have seen, there are many answers to these questions, but one that the early Daoists did not want us to neglect was that empty space in our lives—time simply spent being mindful, watchful, attentive, noticing the world around us and the things our children are doing—constitutes a form of time that gives us rest in a world that tries to busy us with activities. This is why the text of the *Daodejing* urges, "Be active, but have no activities."[13] When we choose to stop and watch our children, we are stopping; we are acting by being mindful, but in an effortless way—in a way that does not involve activities or exertion. It involves being present to and with, but not doing. "In pursuit of the Way, one does less each day; One does less and less until one does nothing; One does nothing yet nothing is left undone."¹⁴ Indeed, there is much to be gained from mindfulness, even when it seems like one is doing nothing. From a Daoist perspective, we benefit from being able to stop, attend, and reflect. The Confucians believed that it was good for our relationships with our children and others, but the Daoists emphasize that it is also a form of rest, which is particularly good for us as parents. "Stop up the openings; Close the gates; to the end of one's life one will remain unperturbed. Unstop the openings; Multiply your activities; And to the end of one's life one will be beyond salvation. To discern the minute is called 'enlightenment.' "¹⁵ Enlightened parenting, from a Daoist standpoint, is seen in attending to our children in the quiet moments, discerning even the small things through attentiveness and reflection. As the *Daodejing* puts it, "The great undertakings in the world all begin with what is small."¹⁶

The text of the *Daodejing* repeatedly emphasizes the importance of stillness and simplicity in our lives: "Without desire and still, the world will settle itself."¹⁷ Another dimension to "waiting time" at children's activities and playgrounds is that it presents an opportunity for stillness and, therefore, renewal. The lives of parents are full—so often, they are too full, with little time to ourselves. But how do we spend the time we are given? The *Daodejing* suggests that we will function better—and be better parents—if we allow room for empty space in our lives. "Thirty spokes are joined in the hub of a wheel. But only by relying on what is not there, do we have the use of the carriage."[18] The empty space that we are given, though, must not be filled with technology—which encourages further busyness, and not genuine stillness. Although he lived in the fourth century BCE, Zhuangzi could have been a twenty-first-century parent when he wrote, "The race is run at a gallop and nothing can stop it. Isn't it sad? Your whole life slaving away and never seeing the completion of your labors. Exhausted, you drudge and slave away without knowing where to turn for rest."[19] From a Daoist perspective, mindfulness—attending to and appreciating the world around us—has a therapeutic effect on us. It is a way of finding rest when there is not time for a nap. Times when we are waiting are opportunities to practice mindfulness.

What happens when we pay attention to our children during the practices, classes, and lessons that strike us as mundane? For one thing, as we have seen, you can learn a lot by watching your child—things that may help you to be a better parent to your child. But it is important to point out here that this is not just a means to an end, but also an end in itself: it is not just that we want to acquire as much information as possible about our children in order to help them to become something or to achieve in certain areas; additionally, the joy in being a parent is taking joy in learning about your child.

Playing with our children also presents opportunities. A friend of mine described watching his brother-in-law play *Star Wars* action figures with his kids, and because he was really playing *with* them, he was able to shape the game in positive ways. One child was being very aggressive and violent in his play, but his dad turned it into a more positive rescue game, where they helped the stormtrooper escape from various predicaments, rather than try to destroy him. When we play with our kids, they play with us, and by being with them, we can help them to become kinder, gentler people.

There is also a unique opportunity when we are not interacting with but observing our children in different settings—an opportunity for our children, because we can learn more about them and, ideally, be better parents by virtue of knowing them better, but also an opportunity for us as parents to take and savor the joy of having children to watch. Mindfulness, in the Confucian and Daoist traditions, has everything to do with seeing your life—including the people in it—as gifts. Attending to and savoring the people and things that are a part of our lives gives rise to joy and to gratitude—which are both robust parts of a fulfilling, flourishing life.

What, then, would Confucian and Daoist philosophers have us do? For one thing, Confucian philosophers encourage us to see ourselves as engaged in a particular craft—the craft of parenting. We are patient farmers, tending sprouts, day in and day out, and this task requires attentiveness. We are to make ourselves students of this task, just as great artisans do. The Confucian *Analects* tells us, "The various artisans dwell in their workshops in order to perfect their crafts, just as the cultivated person learns in order to follow the Way."[20] From the perspective of ancient Chinese philosophers, a key way of doing this is to practice mindfulness. Determine to notice what lies beneath the surface. Resolve to find the joy in the everyday. A central part of this is to recognize that you are not engaged in an unending task. Your children will grow, and never again will they be at precisely the same stage they are in a given moment. There is much to be savored; don't let it pass by without giving a second look, let alone a first glance.

4

Uprooted Sprouts and the Dao of Learning

One must work at it, but do not aim at it directly. Let the heart not forget, but do not help it grow. Do not be like the man from Song. Among the people of the state of Song there was one who, concerned lest his grain not grow, pulled on it. Wearily, he returned home, and said to his family, "Today I am worn out. I helped the grain to grow." His son rushed out and looked at it. The grain was withered. Those in the world who do not help the grain to grow are few.

—MENCIUS

In any village there are sure to be those who are as loyal and trustworthy as I am, but is there anyone who matches my love for learning?

—CONFUCIUS

Love is at the root of everything—all learning, all parenting, all relationships—love, or the lack of it.

—FRED ROGERS

// used to love those books," a friend of mine remarked wistfully, as she spied the *Sweet Valley Twins* books piled in the box I'd recently rescued from my parents' basement. Sorting through the various series of books I read growing up was like seeing old friends again, and I was ready to store them in my own basement in the hope that my own children would one day enjoy them. But my friend marveled at the fact that I seemed to have almost the whole series. "My mom stopped buying those for me when I was ten, because she decided that she only wanted me to read classics. I had to borrow them from friends on the sly in order to keep reading them!" I was taken aback. My parents' approach, throughout the entirety of my childhood, was to let me devour any and every book I wished to read; there were certainly no rules about what I *couldn't* read. My friend and I reminisced about how much we had loved reading as children. For me, this grew into a lifelong love of reading. Even in my early days of college, when I was still a music major, humanities classes were always my favorites. Why? Because of the books. Eventually, I would build my career around many of those books (especially those that were written in classical Chinese). In contrast, my friend's love of reading seemed to simply dissolve. She didn't enjoy any of the classics that her mother prescribed for her. She avoided humanities classes in college and ended up on a very different career path—one that she enjoys, but one that does not involve books.

Without a doubt, many different things influenced our divergent paths. But one of them was our parents' differing approaches to books. Her mother's intentions were good: she loved her daughter and wanted to nurture her love of reading by encouraging her to read great literature, but she didn't realize that pushing her daughter to read only classics could play a role in uprooting—rather than nurturing—a love of literature. And this is why every time I read the story of the man from Song who tugged on his sprouts to try to make them grow and accidentally uprooted them, I wonder if my friend's story is a contemporary retelling of it. Indeed, the story of the uprooted sprouts raises a number of key questions for parents: What happens when we push our children too hard to achieve in certain ways? How can we encourage our children to grow without pushing them in ways that may be harmful, especially in a culture that defines success narrowly and values achievement? In a time when the phrase "helicopter parenting" is widely known, this question has never been more important.

IMPATIENCE AND COMPETITION

Even in ancient China, the problem of pushing too hard was a common one. Mencius says, "Those in the world who do not help the grain to grow are few." Using the sprout metaphor, he distinguishes between two types of problems when it comes to nurturing our children: "Those who abandon the sprouts, thinking their efforts will not help, are those who do not weed their grain. Those who help it grow are those who pull on the grain. Not only does this not help, but it even harms it."[1] This last remark is interesting: Mencius outright rejects the idea that pushing or tugging on the sprouts is helpful. Of course, metaphorically, this is obvious to us: Who tugs on fragile sprouts? All of us *know* that is not going to help them grow. But when we extend this metaphor to our roles as parents, it isn't so clear. What constitutes tugging on the sprouts? When are we in danger of harming our children—of uprooting their love of reading, for instance—as opposed to nurturing them?

A variety of passages in the text of the Mencius are helpful to consider here. The story of the man from Song tugging on his sprouts is a story about impatience. It is about trying to make something happen too soon and too quickly. If we think of my friend's story as a contemporary retelling, then we might notice that encouraging your children to read classics is not in itself a bad thing. But expecting your child to read *only* classics, at quite an early age, is problematic. By contrast, I did read classics, but I read them later. All children are different, of course, and some children might take to classics very early. But that's not what happened here, and Mencius presents us with an interesting opportunity to reflect on when and how early we expect our children to do certain things. We live in a vicious culture when it comes to this matter. There is a notable desire for children to do things earlier and earlier, and a bizarre competition that tends to ensue between parents of young children concerning "milestones." When I first became a mother, I felt self-conscious and, frankly, stressed out about these milestones. Other parents with children of similar ages would brag about how their children were rolling over, then sitting up, then crawling, then walking, and eventually, toilet trained. It continues when they start school, with milestones such as learning how to write, draw, and read. Over time, though, I began to notice something: it mattered greatly to everyone when their child hit one of these milestones. But after your child had hit a milestone, it no longer mattered at all. In time, no one remembered or cared whose child crawled first, was toilet trained first, or who learned to read first. None of it predicted their talents or strengths (and what exactly would early toilet training predict?).

Therefore, one of the key lessons that the man from Song story can teach us is to actively resist impatience and the corresponding tendency to push things to happen before children are ready. Another voice from ancient China that supports this view is the early Daoist Zhuangzi. He would be keen to highlight the often bizarre nature of the priorities we have, and how fixated we become on them. Why do we want our children to be *first*? In some cases, such as potty training, there are clear practical gains such as reducing the cost of diapers and the work of changing them, but in so many other cases, it simply isn't clear that we have good reasons to want our children to achieve something first. Why should we be so eager for our young children to read and write? Is it because we want to take credit for their achievement, to be praised by their teachers for the fact that our children have attained these skills? The evidence on early childhood development simply does not support the view that the credit is ours to take. In truth, there is a complex relationship between nature and nurture, and while parental support is undoubtedly critical, it is not the only factor in a child's development in various areas. Indeed, it can be liberating for parents to learn what scientific studies show: that when it comes to certain milestones, children are not significantly affected by their environment when it comes to when they will, for instance, begin to walk—as long as they have the opportunity to move around and explore safely.

One reason to push back against the tendency to push children to master certain skills too early is that it can do harm to both children and parents. Those who choose alternative educational paths for their children have some interesting insights here. The unschooling movement—an extreme approach to homeschooling that involves significantly less formal instruction at home—has gained popularity, and also resonates in fascinating ways with what early Daoist philosophers would recommend if our children's education were up to them. Emphasis is placed on autonomy over structure, and the philosophy rests on the view that children are natural learners, meaning they do not need to be—and do not learn best when they are—confined to a classroom. One father who takes this unconventional and unstructured approach in educating his sons noted in an interview that his two sons learned to read at ages eight and nine—much later, of course, than most American children who attend public school. Of course, there is no evidence to suggest that earlier is better when it comes to reading or that early reading predicts later strengths in reading. Yet as he puts it, "Even though we did not sit down and teach reading, we read to our children ceaselessly. We immersed our kids in books, and they just picked it up." He goes on to push back against traditional views of what should be taught: "I have nothing against Shakespeare but you might ask why it's not just as important for our kids to be able to go out and identify every tree in the forest outside the house? We believe in the value of our kids knowing their way in the natural world. . . . I think that is where some of the most meaningful experiences would come from." When asked if his kids are missing certain things, he replies, honestly, "Of course. There seems to be a first world belief that we need to expose our kids to as much as we possibly can. The reality is that everything we expose them to is a choice that will effectively deny them exposure to something else."[2]

These are interesting remarks to consider for many reasons. To begin, having seen both of my two older children struggle to learn to read, the idea of children being given the time to learn to read on their own, without the tremendous stress and pressure to meet certain benchmarks, seems very appealing. It would not only have lowered my children's stress levels considerably, but also mine as well. I am not quite ready to join the unschooling movement, but I do think it gives us a ripe opportunity to reflect on our own practices, and just how much we are drawn toward pushing our children before they are ready, and what that sort of pushing can do not only to our children but also to us. Since every child, parent, and family are unique, the answers will be different in different cases. But a part of what Mencius invites us to consider is how harmful it can be when we are too impatient and push too hard, too soon. It is also worth noting how this father's remarks push back against some of the standards that we uncritically accept, including what is included in a curriculum, what the goals of including some things rather than others are, and that fact that any curriculum prioritizes certain skills and activities and excludes others. He notes in particular that some of the most meaningful experiences come from acquaintance with nature—and the interest there is in leading a meaningful life, as opposed to seeking wealth, social status, or prestige.

The latter is a key point that early Chinese philosophers would want parents to focus on as we consider our impatience with our children's development. One reason why we want our children to be first is that we want our children to succeed. But from the perspective of Confucian and Daoist philosophers alike, we ought to be skeptical of our culture's definition of success as it relates to prestige.

What is the trouble with wanting your child to be selected by prestigious programs, schools and, eventually, employers? It is not often that the potential harm of this view is laid bare for us to examine. In an unflinchingly honest editorial, Michael Roth, president of Wesleyan University, did his best to articulate how it manifests in college applications: "It's a dismal learning trajectory: The point of high school is to get into the college that rejects the highest percentage of its applicants; the point of college is to gain access to employers or graduate programs that turn away the greatest number of qualified candidates; the point of life is to have more of the stuff that other people are unable to acquire. What a sorry, soul-killing lesson this is: to value things only to the extent that other people are deprived of them."[3]

DIFFERENT GOALS

In early Confucian texts, we find a markedly different picture of the point of life and learning. Again and again, Confucius says that wealth and prestige undermine, rather than constitute or measure, happiness and fulfillment in life. He rejects outward appearances like "a clever tongue and fine appearance" as measures of success, instead focusing on virtues like gratitude and being humane. He explicitly states that although wealth and social eminence are things that all people desire, he finds them valuable only when people have achieved them by living good lives—

lives in accordance with the Way—defined by the pursuit of virtue, practicing rituals, and giving freely and generously of oneself and what one has to others.[4] Confucius also addresses the *competitiveness* that lies behind what Roth described above, and which also partly motivated my friend's mother to restrict her daughter's reading. Confucianist and Daoist philosophers would reject today's competitive parenting techniques. Confucius argues that we should not strive to be known by others, but to be people *worthy* of being known, instead of concerning ourselves with whether we know others.[5]

He is perfectly transparent about the fact that in his time—very much like ours—wealth and prestige are things that all people desire. The point, for Confucius, is not so much that people *do* desire them—although this is necessary for us to acknowledge if we are to come to terms with the hidden assumptions that we tend to absorb uncritically from our culture and society. Rather, he is most interested in what we should desire instead, and why. If wealth and prestige are not our goals, then what should our goals be? For Confucius, wealth and prestige simply do not lead to our flourishing—and he is happy to discuss individual flourishing as well as that of families, communities, and the wider society of which we are a part. This is because in his view, human flourishing—including our fulfillment, satisfaction, happiness and overall well-being—is the only compelling reason to pursue certain goals in life. And he contends that wealth and prestige do not contribute to our flourishing; indeed, he argues that they often *undermine* it. Now, it is important to understand that Confucius is not talking about a modest level of material comfort, nor is he talking about those who are respected and admired by those who know them; his teachings make abundantly clear that he understands that most people must have a basic level of material well-being in order to flourish, and that others are, generally, drawn to good people. Rather, he is talking about *wealth* and *worldly prestige*—in other words: *fame*. Now, he is careful in how his remarks target these things so as not to condemn people who have acquired them by living a good life. But note the following passage, for example, in which Confucius says, "Eating plain food and drinking water, having only your bent arm as a pillow—certainly there is joy to be found in this! Wealth and eminence attained improperly concern me no more than floating clouds."[6]

Just as we can inadvertently uproot our children's sprouts while trying to get them to grow, we also sometimes transmit values that are not, in reality, in line with our deepest beliefs and intuitions. Most of us know deep down that money and prestige do not make you happy or fulfilled. But we often behave as if we think they do. Indeed, Harvard's Making Caring Common project found a major gap between what parents told researchers they valued in their children, and what children in middle school and high school believed their parents cared about. While 96 percent of parents said moral character was "essential" in their children, more than 80 percent of teens said their parents most valued achievement or personal happiness.[7] From a Confucian perspective, the remedy to this problem is more reflection on what we believe, and how it aligns with what we actually say and do. Mencius believed that reflection helps our moral sensibilities to develop and grow. As he puts it, "The job of the heart-mind is to reflect. If it reflects then it will get Virtue. If it does not reflect, then it will not get it."[8] Part of what is striking about Michael Roth's earlier analysis of the appeal of a degree from a prestigious university is that he unpacks the hidden desires that motivate us. As is the case with good philosophy, it is deeply uncomfortable. (Socrates's persistent questioning and unpacking of people's hidden assumptions and motives famously led to his trial and death.)

But one of the things that makes Chinese philosophers distinctive is that, unlike Socrates, they were not only interested in unearthing the truth, but also in where that gets us. For early Confucian philosophers like Mencius, reflection on what our real beliefs, desires, and motivations are is only a first step. Mencius was also profoundly optimistic about our true feelings. This is why he uses the metaphor of sprouts to describe our natural goodness; it needs to be nurtured, but it is very much there in the first place. Mencius would argue that the same is true of us as parents. Even when we are seduced by the appeal of a prestigious university, wanting our children to go further than others, this is done out of love for our children. Mencius would especially focus on the fact that when we stop and reflect, we find that we do not really believe that money and prestige will lead our children to have fulfilled, meaningful, happy lives. We are easily seduced by a culture in which that view is marketed to us continuously— as it was in Mencius's time, as well—but deep down, we know it is not true. Take a minute and think of the most wealthy, famous, and powerful people you know. Now, take another minute and think of the people you would most like your children to grow up to be like. Consider how different those two lists are.

Being more aware of what we truly believe can and does lead us to behave differently. (You may wonder if the outcome might have been different if someone had asked the man from Song *why* he wanted his sprouts to grow more quickly, and whether he really believed that tugging on them would help.) But it also takes work to change the way we think, talk, and behave. One of the key ways in which parents can resist impatience and the urge to force sprouts to grow more quickly is to take a step back and recognize that much of what seems urgently important now, will not be important at all later—and in fact is wholly unimportant in the grand scheme of things. The early Daoist philosopher Zhuangzi tells the story of a monkey trainer to illustrate this. "When the monkey trainer was passing out nuts he said, 'You get three in the morning and four at night.' The monkeys were all angry. 'All right,' he said, 'you get four in the morning and three at night.' The monkeys were all pleased."[9] For Zhuangzi, we are those monkeys. We tend to be delighted by having our child do something first, and troubled when they are last. Just as the monkeys all receive the same number of nuts in a day but are vexed by how many nuts they are receiving *right now*, we tend to be vexed by what our children are doing *right now*, failing, just like those monkeys, to recognize that it won't matter in the long run. (Of course, not hitting milestones within a "normal" range can sometimes be an early indicator of a disability. But pediatricians emphasize the large window for most milestones, and the need for parents not to place undue weight on such things. As one pediatrician puts it, "A child with a gross motor delay may always be clumsy or he may turn out to be a Heisman trophy winner. A child with an expressive language delay may turn out to have a learning disability or she may become valedictorian."[10])

In addition to the issue of impatience, though, it is important not to miss the fact that the farmer *uprooted his sprouts*. He did more than harm them: he destroyed them completely. Mencius emphasizes this repeatedly in order to emphasize how susceptible we are to harm and damage as children. In another metaphor-rich parable, Mencius again offers a picture of fragile sprouts that are demolished: "The trees of Ox Mountain were once beautiful. But because it bordered on a large state, hatchets and axes besieged it. Could it remain verdant? Due to the rest it got during the day or night, and the moisture of the rain and dew, it was not that there were no sprouts or shoots growing there. But oxen and sheep then came and grazed on them. Hence, it was as if it were barren. People, see-

ing it barren, believed that there had never been any tim-
ber there."[11]

When my friend told me about her mother's demand
that she read only classics and no other books, she wasn't
describing an isolated incident. Her mother was fiercely
competitive, always wanting her children to "get ahead"
(of others), and my friend's childhood was littered with
experiences of this sort. This is why, although it is more
comfortable to think that perhaps we were always on different paths, and the differing attitudes, approaches, and
goals of our parents were not decisive, my friend insists
that what happened was formative for her in a critical way.
She loves her mother, but she traces the evaporation of her
love of books to the day her mother instituted the "classics only" policy. We will never know the precise mix of
"nature and nurture" when it comes to each of our lives,
but what Mencius would wish to emphasize is the key
role that parents sometimes play in closing down certain
possibilities for their children. That is not to say that my
friend is unhappy in her career today, or that she would
be happier if had she become a scholar of literature. But as
parents it seems that, whenever possible, one of our basic
goals should be to avoid harming or closing down possibilities for our children. To be sure, due to the limits of time
and resources, none of us can open up every opportunity
in the world for our children. All of us are limited by our
time and place, and by the limits of what we can reasonably do in a day. And all of us will make choices that will
hurt our children sometimes. Learning from Mencius's

metaphors is not about being perfect. It is about doing the best we can. It is about being more aware of our desires, intentions and goals and how they lead us to interact with our children, and of the fragility of our children's "sprouts" and their need for nurturance and encouragement that is gentle and not overbearing. It is about recognizing that even when our intentions are good, the way that we act on them can be harmful when we do too much and push too hard. As Mencius says, "One must work at it, but do not aim at it directly. Let the heart not forget, but do not help it to grow."

A LOVE OF LEARNING

As a remedy to the tendency to push our children too hard, one thing that Confucian philosophers like Mencius would have us do is to think less in terms of following specific rules or practices (e.g., a child must read only classics in order to become a great reader and appreciator of literature) and more in terms of nurturing broad capacities (e.g., the ability to read, a love of reading, and a love of learning). When it comes to nurturing such capacities, Confucian and Daoist philosophers alike emphasize enjoyment of doing over ability or achievement. This is surprising to many who are familiar with East Asian cultures, because although most people are aware that Confucianism is largely responsible for the strong emphasis on learning in these cultures, few are aware that the earliest Confucian views focus primarily on developing a love of learning. Indeed, what Mencius would want to emphasize is that what is often uprooted when we push our children too hard to achieve academically is their *enjoyment* of learning.

Here the Confucian tradition can serve as a surprising resource for today's parents. The early Confucians greatly valued learning and study, which they paired with reflection, emphasizing that "study without reflection is a waste; reflection without study is a danger."[12] This tells us something important: education was not a matter of simply learning information. In the Confucian tradition, it always involved reflection on the meaning of what one learned, why it was important and how it might be applied today. This also involves self-knowledge; Confucius defines wisdom as "recognizing what you know and recognizing what you do not know." True learning involves not just rote memorization or the ability to regurgitate information, but also being able to use and apply what you've learned. This is seen clearly in the Confucian definition of a teacher: "someone who is able to use the past to understand the present." The aim is not to be able to recite classics or history, but to understand why they are worth studying, how they can make us better people, and help us to lead more meaningful, fulfilling lives. Confucians explicitly reject the view that being "learned" is simply about knowledge or academic skills: "Imagine someone who recognizes and admires worthiness and therefore changes his lustful nature, who is able to fully exhaust his strength in serving his parent and extend himself to the utmost in serving his lord, and who is trustworthy in speech when acting with friends and associates. Even if you said of such a person, 'Oh, but he is not learned,' I would still insist that it is precisely such qualities that make one worthy of being called 'learned.'"[13] What we find here is a holistic view of education—one which integrates moral and academic learning, and also stresses the balance between study and reflection on the meaning of what one studies. Considering that these texts were written in the fourth and third centuries BCE, that is remarkably progressive.

Most surprising, however, is that when it comes to learning, ancient Confucians talked more about the importance of developing a *love* of learning than anything else. And while they always hoped and believed that when a child develops a real love of learning, they will go on to learn much and to learn well, their emphasis on developing a love of learning came first. Here, children's *feelings* about learning are prioritized. For Mencius and for the early Daoists, children have a natural love of and inclination to learn. This is seen in their curiosity and inquisitiveness about everything around them, and in the genuine joy they take in engaging with—and learning about—the world. When Confucius praises his most gifted student, it was not for his knowledge or ability, but for his love of learning.[14] He also maintains that a love of learning serves as a necessary complement to all of the other virtues: "Loving Goodness without balancing it with a love for learning will result in the vice of foolishness. Loving wisdom without balancing it with a love for learning will result in the vice of deviance. Loving trustworthiness without balancing it with a love for learning will result in the vice of harmful rigidity. . . ."[15] (A love of nature, too, must be balanced with a love for learning. If you just express a love of the natural world but don't really learn about it, you don't really understand what is loveable—and in some cases dangerous—about it.) Once again, we see that the experience of true joy—seen here in loving to learn—is a central part of what Confucians would have us strive for as parents.

If we genuinely take to heart what ancient Confucian texts tell us about learning, we will be more concerned about our children's feelings about and attitudes toward learning instead of focusing inordinately on their academic achievements. Again, these two are not necessarily opposed to each other, but in practice they often are. When parents push too hard for their children to achieve in certain ways, they sometimes inadvertently uproot children's natural curiosity and the beginnings of a love of learning. When a child acquires a skill, takes an interest in something, or shows a particular aptitude for it, we are often inclined to ask how we can help our child get better at it. Confucian philosophers would have parents ask a different question: What can I do to help my child to continue to take joy in this activity?

They also, however, would urge us to attend very closely to what children enjoy, and always begin there. There are a variety of ways in which this might have impact on modern parenting. For one, parents will focus more on the *process* of learning—and finding ways for children to take joy in it—than the end result. This means attending closely to the things our children enjoy learning about and doing, and then building on them. In turn, we should accept that they will not always do the things we might choose or that other children are doing. And one of the things *that* means is that we will sometimes rely more on others—friends, teachers, family members—to help our children cultivate interests in areas that lie outside of our interests and background.

This is just as much about cultivating a love of learning as seeing ourselves as part of a collective, as opposed to individualistic, endeavor to educate our children. It is not an incidental part of Mencius's sprout metaphors that they are *agricultural* metaphors, as opposed to merely botanical metaphors. Mencius was a Confucian, and Confucian philosophers always emphasize that we grow and are nurtured in human communities, just as Mencius's sprouts are tended by farmers—not growing wild in nature. (The latter metaphor was one that Daoist philosophers tended to favor more.) Mencius also emphasized that we, as parents alone, cannot do all that needs to be done for our children. There will be times that teachers, friends, grandparents, or other family members will see the need for a little more water, a little more sunlight or shade, or fertilizer in the soil. And there will be times when they are in a better position than we are to provide those things. We need others to assist in the process of tending the sprouts.

The unique role of teachers in relation to our children's development should not be overlooked, for this was something that deeply interested Confucians throughout their history. In a previous chapter, we saw that Mencius's mother was finally satisfied when she found a home that was next to a school, and Mencius began to imitate the activities of the teachers. Confucians always emphasized and valued the importance of teachers. And an added insight from the Confucian tradition—and one that is also seen in some parts of contemporary East Asia—is that if we truly value education and learning, then we ought to value teachers more highly. Yet teachers in America today do not enjoy the same kind of prestige as many other professions—nor do they receive the pay they deserve. Confucians valued teachers because they cared about the process and experience of *learning*—and the way that it could transform our character—as opposed to simply seeing learning as a means to certain forms of achievement or to a higher-paying job.

There is much here for us to reflect on in our own attitudes and practices, and there is much that parents can do, at a practical level, to more highly value and express gratitude to their children's teachers. Parents might start by letting the principal know when a teacher has done a particularly good job with something. (It's important to let principals know when we are grateful for *their* efforts, too.) It is more common to complain when something is wrong than to offer praise when something is done exceptionally well, and this is relatively easy to correct simply by writing a note, sending an email, or making a phone call. Additionally, taking the time to write teachers to tell them when and how they have positively affected a child goes a long way. Most teachers go into teaching because they want to make a difference. It's important to tell them when they do. As we saw earlier in this book, Chinese philosophers stress that it is often the simplest gestures, seen in their "rituals," that make the biggest difference. I was surprised when one of my son's teachers thanked me for a note I'd written to her, telling me, "You don't understand. We don't get notes like that." It surprised me not only because she is a very popular teacher, but also because I know that parents at our school give gifts to teachers throughout the year. But for most of us, it means a great deal to hear that the things we have done have been noticed and appreciated, and the only way for us to express that adequately is in words. For parents, this is a matter of time and priorities. But from a Confucian standpoint, it is time well spent.

Parents also need to work at seeing themselves as part-ners and allies with their child's teachers. This means working to avoid wholly delegating the task of a child's education to others—including teachers, tutors, and nan-nies. The more parents sit down and work with their chil-dren on schoolwork, generally speaking, the more they will be able to understand teachers' concerns, reinforce the things teachers are working to achieve with their chil-dren, and, in some cases, correct mistaken impressions that teachers might have. It also means being open to and even expecting that teachers may help you to discover something new about your child, or they may notice something you haven't, and not being threatened by that; you must recognize that sending your child to school introduces a variety of people who can help your child to realize her potential. Of course, it is easier to make some teachers your allies than others—teachers, too, have varying levels of experience, different strengths and weaknesses, and different personalities. Some teachers will be better matches for your child than others. Some school years will be better than others. But it remains important for us to work at seeing ourselves as part of a "village"—and to see our own parenting as part of a larger collective endeavor to nurture our children's growth and development.

⚜ 5 ⚜

Sprouts, Not Seeds:
The Dao of Nature
and Nurture

Human nature's being good is like water's tending downward. There is no human who does not tend toward goodness.

—MENCIUS

People's nature is bad. Their goodness is a matter of deliberate effort.

—XUNZI

When my sons were babies, I would stare at them and wonder what, precisely, stared back.

—PAUL BLOOM, *Just Babies:
The Origins of Good and Evil*

Without knowing it, the Yale Baby Lab has conducted a series of experiments that recommend the study of ancient Chinese philosophy to parents today. A five-month-old watches as one puppet struggles to lift the lid on a box. Another puppet comes and helps, opening the lid all the way. In the next scene, the first puppet once again struggles to open the box, but this time, a third puppet comes and jumps on the box, slamming it shut. After the puppet show, when asked which puppet they like, more than three-fourths of babies tested reached for the "nice" puppet. What about for three-month-olds? They, too, overwhelmingly preferred the "nice" puppet. The study was replicated again and again, with infants of varying ages, different puppets, and different scenarios. The statistical trend was not subtle. A substantial body of evidence suggests that our children are born with a basic sense of right and wrong—seen in both the tendency to like individuals who are helpful and kind, and in the tendency to dislike those who are unkind.[1] But what does this mean for us as parents? Should it guide what—and how—we teach our children? Chinese philosophers certainly thought so.

Long before we had baby labs and controlled studies, and long before Western philosophers like Hobbes, Rousseau, and Hume offered theories of human nature, Chinese philosophers in the fourth and third centuries BCE were debating whether our children start out with good tendencies or bad tendencies. Mencius was born after Confucius died, but he taught, practiced, and defended Confucius's teachings as best he could. He spent much of his career traveling from state to state, meeting with rulers, in hopes of influencing their policies so that people would recover the traditional Confucian rituals and values that had once made their society strong and humane. He thought that if people would just pay attention to human nature, following the Confucian Way would become much easier. Mencius believed that human nature is good, and, you'll recall, he used the metaphor of tender sprouts and shoots growing in a field to represent that goodness. For Mencius, we have natural moral tendencies that are the beginnings of virtues like compassion, but although these tendencies are visible and active, like sprouts, they are also fragile and can easily be harmed by any number of environmental factors: too much or too little rain or sunlight, garden pests, hungry deer or overanxious farmers, or weeds that steal nutrients. Just ask any farmer or gardener—the list is practically endless.

Even though Mencius talked about the ways in which sprouts can be damaged, and the many kinds of support and nurturance they still require, his fellow Confucian philosopher Xunzi nevertheless found this view too optimistic. Xunzi lived after Mencius and was the leading Confucian scholar of his day. He held high office at one point, but in his teaching and writings he hoped to help his society by influencing his students, many of whom were planning on careers in government. Looking at humanity, he simply did not agree that we start out life with anything like moral tendencies. Xunzi rejected Mencius's account of human nature, arguing instead that human nature is bad. But he did not claim that human nature is *evil*. We are not, in his view, naturally inclined to *enjoy* doing the wrong thing, or to intentionally reject what we know is right. Rather, for Xunzi, we are naturally selfish, and we start out morally blind. We have no internal moral compass. For him, this means that human nature is bad: we start out without the beginnings of any virtues or any moral inclinations whatsoever. And that is not a pretty picture.

Although Mencius and Xunzi disagreed over whether human nature was primarily good or bad, they agreed on a few fundamentals: (1) How we start out in life matters greatly for parents because it can help us to do a better job of nurturing qualities like kindness, generosity, gratitude, resilience, and persistence in our children. Understanding our children's nature, then, can help us to nurture the qualities that will lead them to become happy and fulfilled people. (2) Our nature is changeable. We can be cultivated—every part of us, from our behaviors and habits, both large and small, all the way down to our attitudes, emotions, intentions, and motives. Mencius intentionally chose the metaphor of sprouts and not seeds for precisely this reason: sprouts are active, dynamic, and changeable. Xunzi, too, believed that the most important part of our nature is that we are changeable, which is why his metaphors include substances like wood and clay, which can be carved or reshaped.

The latter claim is something that separates early Chinese philosophers from many traditional Western philosophers. Thomas Hobbes, for instance, did not believe that we could ever fundamentally change our nature as humans. Rather, it had to be managed by setting up the rules of society in the right way. The philosopher Philip J. Ivanhoe uses the helpful illustration of a game: for philosophers like Hobbes, we are a little like chess pieces, whose powers are fixed. All we can do is learn to manage and manipulate the pieces better.[2] Hobbes argues that we should use humans' natural fear of a sovereign ruler to maintain order: we can't change our natural human tendency to be fearful, so we must harness that fear to help create a stable society. (In his autobiography, Hobbes famously writes, "Fear and I were born twins," since on the day of his birth Hobbes's mother went into premature labor after being terrified by the news that the Spanish Armada had set sail to attack England.) In contrast, Mencius and Xunzi believed that we could change the powers that we are born with. They believed that we could cultivate and change both our behavior as well as our feelings, desires, intentions, and attitudes, so that we can not only reliably behave respectfully toward others, but also actually *feel* and be motivated by respect, reverence, and gratitude.

Additionally, and unlike many traditional Western philosophers, Mencius and Xunzi were interested in human nature not primarily because they wanted to know the truth or believed that we should know the truth (because knowing the truth is good and important, in and of itself), but because they thought that understanding human nature would help us to live better lives. Put another way, their aims were mainly therapeutic, not theoretical. They didn't believe that we could really succeed at the task of moral self-cultivation if we didn't understand where we started out. For Confucian philosophers like Mencius and Xunzi, and for early Daoist philosophers as well, this would be a bit like trying to give a friend directions to your home without knowing where she was coming from. Whether we are looking at a map or our GPS, where must we begin? With our starting point. Following this analogy a bit further, we see that Mencius and Xunzi were deeply interested not only in where we started but also in what the terrain was like on the journey. Will our final destination be on the right or the left? Is it on a divided highway or at the end of a gravel road? Do we have to climb a twisting mountain path or coast along a gradual slope stretching toward the sea? How hard is the journey, and how far? All of this matters for how we will travel—by foot, by bike, or by car? And as all parents know, it affects the most important question of all: How many snacks will we need to pack?

HUMAN NATURE AND THE
CULTIVATION OF CHILDREN

Despite the fact that they thought we all shared a common human nature, all of the early Chinese philosophers I discuss in this book believed that each child is unique. Indeed, this was the inspiration for Confucian views of harmony, which they viewed as the highest cultural achievement. From a Confucian perspective, harmony is the proper goal of any family, community, and society. By harmony they absolutely did not mean uniformity, and they emphasized this by using the metaphors of music and food. The most beautiful music involves harmony—different and complementary notes sung or played together simultaneously—not just in unison (singing or playing the same note together). Likewise, the most delicious dish is one that includes multiple flavors blending together in a complementary way—as the best Chinese food does. This is what a family, community, and society ought to be like, according to early Confucian philosophers, and it is a view that takes seriously—and values—the differences between us. Confucians, then, did not aim to change all of the natural differences between children, but to help us see how they might lead to a harmonious family, which is something more beautiful than a family where everyone has precisely the same strengths and weaknesses. Difference, from an early Confucian perspective, can yield the best type of family. Thus, differences are affirmed and developed. The Daoist tradition, too, emphasizes that each of us has distinctive gifts and tendencies, and as we shall see, these differences—even if they include disabilities—are to be celebrated and developed, not removed.

I stress this because any account of human nature that neglects the very real differences between different children is clearly problematic, as parents who have multiple children can attest. There are constitutional differences between individual children from the time they are born as well as differences connected to gender, and there are wide-ranging views and sharp disagreements among parents, especially regarding the latter. (I cannot count the times we heard "Boys are easier" when we found out our first child would be a boy—most often from people who only had sons. But many of my friends with both sons and daughters laughed hysterically when they heard that. Indeed, one friend with a daughter and a son once remarked that perhaps Mencius thought human nature was good because he had daughters, and Xunzi thought human nature was bad because he had sons.) The reality is that each child is different, measuring the "ease" or "difficulty" of a child is complicated, and children change as they grow—just as we grow and change as parents. As an infant, our son learned to fall asleep on his own very easily and was an excellent sleeper. Our older daughter was just the opposite, and none of the approaches that had worked easily for our son seemed to help. As they grew, they switched: our son began to struggle with sleep, and our daughter became the best sleeper in the family. A friend of mine loves to tell the story of what an easy, laid-back baby their oldest child was, and how they thought it was all because they knew just what to do as parents. Then their second child was born, and the things they had done for their first child didn't work at all. Children have different dispositions, strengths, and challenges—many of which are with them from birth, and are not the result of what we have or have not done.

Early Chinese philosophers believed that in the midst of these types of differences, we still share a common moral nature, just as we share a common physical nature. As Mencius put it, "People having these four sprouts is like their having four limbs."[3] Now, that is not to deny the reality of rare physical disabilities—not everyone is born with four limbs, and that is something early Chinese philosophers were aware of and wrote about, too, as we shall see—nor is it to deny that some humans seem to lack the basic moral sensibilities or capacities that most of us have. But for Mencius, this is how most of us are. And if most of us share basic tendencies but are also different in a variety of ways, this makes studying our children's natures—not just our shared human nature but the natural tendencies of each child—all the more important.

Mencius writes that "humans all have hearts that are not unfeeling toward others," and goes on to offer a story to explain what he means: "Suppose someone suddenly saw a child about to fall into a well: everyone in such a situation would have a feeling of alarm and compassion—not because one sought to get in good with the child's parents, not because one wanted fame among their neighbors and friends, and not because one would dislike the sound of the child's cries."[4] The philosopher Bryan Van Norden stresses that Mencius does *not* say everyone in this situation would try to save the child; rather, Mencius's claim is solely about the feelings people would have.[5] Everyone would *feel* alarm and compassion. He also anticipates a series of objections—that perhaps people would only feel this way because they wanted to show concern or act heroically to earn prestige, or because they wanted to get that annoying crying to stop. Mencius presents these objections as laughable because he finds them wholly uncompelling. It is clear that the alarm and compassion people would feel tells us something about our humanity. He goes on to list the four moral tendencies that he thinks we are all born with and notes, too, the virtues that they grow into with the proper nurturance: compassion (the "sprout" that grows into benevolence), disdain (the sprout that grows into righteousness), deference (the sprout of ritual propriety), and approval and disapproval (the sprout of wisdom). He seeks to stress their rudimentary nature as well as their strength, noting that "having these four sprouts within oneself, if one knows how to fill them all out, it will be like a fire starting up, a spring breaking through!"

Especially noteworthy are the words "if one knows how to fill them all out." In other words, *if* the sprouts get the right protection, nourishment, and cultivation from human hands, then they will grow. He goes on to say that if these natural moral tendencies flourish, it will lead one to show compassion for all—even strangers. But if, on the other hand, they don't develop, a person will not even care for her own parents.[6] This is a stunning claim for a Confucian. Mencius and other Confucians believed that the most fundamental relationship for all of us is our relationship with our parents, and that some degree of love and affection comes naturally in this relationship. But Mencius acknowledges here that some people do not treat their parents with love and respect, and he seeks to relate that to his theory of human nature. This is important, because the key objection one can make is that Mencius is excessively optimistic, and fails to take account of what goes wrong with people who are obviously not good.

Indeed, Mencius makes this even more explicit, saying that "they can become good. This is what I mean by calling their natures good. As for their becoming not good, this is not the fault of their potential."[7] He tells two stories to illustrate this. He opens the first, the parable of the barley seeds, by noting that "in years of plenty, most young men are gentle; in years of poverty, most young men are cruel," but their potential—their nature as humans—is the same. It is their environment that differs. "Consider barley," he writes. "Sow the seeds and cover them. The soil is the same and the time of planting is also the same. They grow rapidly, and by the time of the summer solstice they have all ripened. Although there are some differences, these are due to the richness of the soil, and to unevenness in the rain and in human effort. Hence, in general, things of the same kind are all similar. Why would one have any doubt about this when it comes to humans alone?" Mencius concludes by saying, "We and the sage are of the same kind."[8] For Mencius, sages and other people that we admire— saints and others who seem truly heroic in their moral capacities—are not, in fact, different from us by nature. We can all become such people by nurturing our moral tendencies—and if others do so for us, especially during the earliest years of our lives.

The therapeutic as opposed to purely theoretical concerns of Chinese philosophers are evident in Xunzi's rejection of Mencius's view. He says outright that he finds Mencius's view dangerous, for in fact there are no moral tendencies within us to serve as our guide. So, if we follow our inner compass, as Mencius would have us do, we will find only our physical desires leading us. And so, he writes, "People's nature is bad. Their goodness is a matter of deliberate effort."[9] "Bad" here means a state of moral blindness, and indeed Xunzi writes that failing to follow teachers and traditions and instead using one's own judgment "is like relying on a blind person to distinguish colors, or like relying on a deaf person to distinguish sounds."[10] Contrary to everything that Mencius argues, in Xunzi's view we simply have no moral sensibilities prior to receiving a moral education.

Xunzi offers a series of alternative metaphors that he thinks capture the true nature of moral development much better than Mencius's sprouts (which are, as we recall, nonexistent in Xunzi's view). As he puts it, "Crooked wood must await steaming and straightening on the shaping frame, and only then does it become straight. Blunt metal must await honing and grinding, and only then does it become sharp."[11] His are the metaphors of determined artisans working with stubborn substances: wood, clay, metal, and stone. Here Xunzi emphasizes the need for us to understand the nature of the journey, and not just how it begins or ends: "Through steaming and bending, you can make wood straight as a plumb line into a wheel. And after its curve conforms to the compass, even when parched under the sun it will not become straight again."[12] Xunzi stresses not only how long and difficult the process of shaping our children's character is, but also that we are seeking to help our children conform to an artificial standard (the wheel)—as opposed to following their natural inclinations. But he contends that not only is complete change possible, it is also permanent. We can completely overcome our original shape, taking on a wholly new shape. Interestingly, Xunzi does not argue that we ought to completely eliminate the desires that lead us prior to moral cultivation; rather, he sees the process of moral cultivation as partly a process of acquiring moral sensibilities and partly a process of channeling and redirecting our desires, just as one might create a channel to redirect water that has pooled on a road so that it drains and doesn't ruin the roadway. Our nonmoral desires are not bad in and of themselves, but they can be very harmful if they are not shaped in the right ways. Xunzi envisions ritual playing a key role in the process of shaping our nature: "Ritual cuts off what is too long and extends what is too short. It subtracts from what is excessive and adds to what is insufficient." Ultimately, Xunzi claims that Mencius's view "does not match the test of experience."[13] At bottom, then, he and Mencius make different observations of what we start out like.

MENCIAN AND XUNZIAN ADVICE
FOR MODERN PARENTS

Standing in the middle of a peach orchard one day, I thought of Mencius. My son was throwing a huge tantrum after we picked fruit at the pick-your-own farm, and I was stumped over what to do to get him to stop. I understood why he was upset, but it wasn't possible to give him what he wanted (a ride back to the parking lot on the tractor). His sister was tired, and people were staring. I had tried all of the best Mencian-style approaches I knew: trying to get him to stop and take deep breaths, to calm down, turn inward and think about how he was feeling and why—all in the name of coaxing out the goodness that I knew resided within him. Sometimes, it worked. But not always, and not this time. After making several different attempts and after considerable time had passed with no progress, I started to think of Xunzi. I couldn't deny that he was at least partly right: there were times, it seemed, when gentle encouragement wasn't what was needed. It was becoming clear that the only path out of the orchard was going to be a bumpy one. That's when I started channeling my inner artisan, determined to reshape a tough lump of clay—in this case, my son's behavior. I started walking. My son kept screaming. I looked back and told him that he needed to follow me. I kept walking. More screaming. I kept him in my sight, but I walked on. He kept screaming, but he followed. He carried on throughout most of the long walk from the orchard back to the car. Finally, he gradually started to calm down. I wish I could end this story by saying "That day, my son learned that you don't get your way by throwing a tantrum." But something that both Mencius and Xunzi get right is that it takes a long time for sprouts to grow, and for clay to take on a new shape.

In parenting, one of the biggest challenges is figuring out which approach will work for your child in any given scenario, whether it is getting them to stop throwing a tantrum, convincing them to do their homework, or helping them to compromise with a friend or sibling. Mencius and Xunzi remind me that different types of responses should be used in different situations. Their colorful metaphors also help me to think about the various kinds of approaches that I can try as a parent. Sometimes, you learn what will work only by trial and error: by first trying the approach of a patient farmer, then the determined artisan, as I did that day in the peach orchard. Other times, we know exactly what we need to do, but the challenge lies in remaining calm and maintaining the resolve to do it. In all of these cases, it can be helpful to think about the task we are engaged in: Is it a matter of gentle encouragement or a matter of reshaping, like an artisan working in a difficult medium? The ability to call to mind Mencian and Xunzian approaches in order to better understand what we must do and bring ourselves to do it effectively can be very helpful in such situations.

In trying to figure out the best ways to help to our children, we still might wonder, who is closer to being right about human nature—Mencius or Xunzi? And does the question of whether we are originally good or bad really matter in parenting? In answering these questions, a good place to begin is precisely where we begin our lives: as infants. Paul Bloom's recent work, *Just Babies: The Origins of Good and Evil*, explores what our best science tells us about human nature, including the work that he and his colleagues have done at the Yale Baby Lab (more formally known as the Yale Infant Cognition Center). These experiments with infants as young as three months, all the way through the various stages of infancy and childhood, suggest that, as Bloom puts it, "some aspects of morality come naturally to us—and others do not. We have a moral sense that enables us to judge others and that guides our compassion. We are naturally kind to others, at least some of the time."[14] Bloom anticipates those who would argue that three-month-olds have already learned morality (arguing for the "nurture" side of the debate) by stressing that "many natural traits don't emerge right away—think of freckles and wisdom teeth and underarm hair. The brain, like the rest of the body, takes time to grow." What he proposes, though, is that certain moral foundations are not the results of "nurture." They are, rather, a part of our nature as human beings.

The question of what our nature is—what tendencies and capacities we start out our lives with—matters greatly when it comes to parenting. This is easiest to observe in relation to children's natural aptitudes. The beloved children's author Tomie dePaola describes how he always loved drawing, from the time he was a very small child. In *The Art Lesson*, he tells the story of his experience with two teachers, one of whom creatively and gently encouraged the natural ability that was already there, while the other insisted that he must conform to what all of the other children did in art class. The former teacher's Mencian-style approach was far more effective. Encouraging and nurturing a child's natural gifts (and not attempting to reshape them in a Xunzian-style way) stands in contrast with what must happen when children face very real struggles. Like dePaola, children's author Patricia Polacco describes how she always loved drawing. But in *Thank You, Mister Falker*, she shares the story of her struggle with dyslexia and her difficulty with reading and math. The teacher who first recognized her disability was also the teacher who recognized her remarkable artistic talent and encouraged her. That gentle nurturing of her artistic ability, which came so naturally to her, stood in contrast to the hard work that was involved in helping her learn to read and do math—where there were no natural tendencies to be encouraged; to the contrary, her disability presented a situation very much like the toughest Xunzian clay or the most severely warped wood, in need of complete and total reshaping. It was possible, but had her teachers not understood how long and difficult the process would be—or if they had thought that she just needed to tap into some natural ability or desire—they would not have succeeded in helping her.

For all children, the acquisition of certain skills normally requires a lot of hard work; this is a much more Xunzian task. At first, the process of learning to ride a bike or play a musical instrument is not usually very much fun because these things don't typically come "naturally"; they involve a lot of practice, failure, and hard work. It's important for children and parents to understand that some tasks are like that: they require lots of hard work because we have to acquire new abilities "from scratch." In other cases, we are nurturing an ability that is already there and just needs the right encouragement to grow and thrive. This was certainly the case for dePaola and Polacco with drawing. And in those cases, taking a more Xunzian approach can be harmful, inadvertently rooting out some of the "sprouts" that are there.

When it comes to helping our kids to become kinder and more caring, generous and grateful, are we encouraging natural moral tendencies that already exist, or are we instilling them from scratch? Are there bad tendencies that we need to redirect or remove? Bloom argues that it is a little of both: there are good tendencies (apparent even in young infants) that need to be encouraged, such as a tendency to feel sympathy for those who are treated poorly and to dislike those who are unkind. The "sprouts" of virtues are seen in the behavior of infants and children in many things, from the fact that infants find crying unpleasant (it tends to make them cry themselves) to the fact that babies and young children don't just turn away from someone who is in pain—they try to make the other person feel better. Bloom points out that babies' and toddlers' attempts at soothing others are far from perfect: they are not as frequent as one would hope, toddlers soothe less than older children, and older children soothe less than adults—something that also affirms Mencius's use of the metaphor of sprouts that are growing, little by little, eventually with the right forms of nurturance growing into reliable dispositions to show compassion and care for others.

On the other hand, some natural tendencies need to be redirected or reshaped, such as the tendency to favor those who are like ourselves, even in superficial ways. Research shows that when presented with a choice between two snacks, and then shown one puppet who chose their preferred snack (and another who chose the alternative snack), even young infants overwhelmingly liked the puppet who chose their preferred snack better than the puppet who did not. Psychologists have long been aware of the same basic tendency in adults—to prefer those with whom we share even the most trivial similarities. This sort of tendency is not a moral tendency; if not redirected or corrected, preferences for those who are like ourselves can be harmful. Note the contrast between disliking those who treat others badly and disliking those who are different from ourselves. The existence of both tendencies has been highlighted repeatedly in study after study. And it tells us much about what we are working with when we are working to help our children to develop virtues like compassion and justice. Our children are not moral blank slates.

Bloom's research suggests that Mencius and Xunzi were both partly right. Mencius was correct that we do possess moral sprouts. The beginnings of compassion, for instance, do reside within us, and as a result our central task as parents is to encourage and nurture those tendencies. But we do not possess the beginnings or sprouts of all of the virtues we need. Some virtues must be fully acquired, and we also have some bad tendencies that need to be reshaped or rooted out.

In her book *The Gardener and the Carpenter*, the psychologist Alison Gopnik uses metaphors that sound much like Mencius's and Xunzi's to critique the tendency of contemporary parents, like carpenters, to focus on turning their children into something very specific: a straight-A student, a doctor, or a lawyer. She argues that our goals should be much more open-ended, and that we should seek to create a protected and nurturing space for children—like gardeners do. We should understand our task as parents as that of gardeners, not carpenters. Although written more than two thousand years later and without any awareness of Mencian and Xunzian views, part of what Gopnik's work shows is how universal their metaphors are. Gopnik's overarching point resonates strongly with the view we have seen in a variety of Chinese philosophers: that we as parents should be more focused on helping our children to flourish as people than on helping them to achieve worldly success. An important difference, though, is that she uses these metaphors in a different way. For Gopnik, carpentry and gardening are metaphors for what parents do, and how fixed their goals are. When Mencius and Xunzi use these and related metaphors, they are not just describing what parents do, but the fundamental character of human nature and the process of moral cultivation—which parents participate in, but that many other people also do (including our children, as they begin to cultivate themselves). Xunzi did not solely focus on carpentry, but more broadly on the task of determined artisans working in a difficult medium—be it wood, clay, metal, or stone—because all of these substances can be shaped into something beautiful, but the process is difficult and requires skill and persistence. And Mencius discussed several different kinds of sprouts in order to emphasize that there is always something that they are meant to become—bean sprouts grow into bean plants, and barley sprouts grow into barley plants. For both Mencius and Xunzi, we are all capable of becoming virtuous in the end. This is why Mencius's sprouts are the sprouts of farmers, not recreational gardeners: they represent something essential that has to be nourished in order for us to flourish, not something that adds additional beauty or enjoyment.

If we bring Xunzi's metaphors into conversation with Bloom's research, we can see how parents can benefit from understanding their task in both Mencian and Xunzian terms. If our focus is on moral cultivation—on helping our children to become kind, caring, and generous—we must nurture some tendencies and reshape others. Therefore, both Mencian and Xunzian approaches can be helpful to parents if we see them as complementary, each offering colorful metaphors for what is needed at different times, and in different endeavors. One of our most important tasks as parents is to look closely and discern, in any given situation, if there is something we need to help preserve or nurture in our children, or something that needs to be instilled or reshaped. It is important to remember that each child is unique, which means that each parent's task will be unique. When our older daughter was in kindergarten, reading was a tremendous struggle for her—sounding out even simple words just made no sense at all to her—but she flourished when it came to her interactions with her peers; she made friends easily in any group of children. Meanwhile, one of my daughter's friends showed great strengths in reading very early—but she wanted to read all the time at school, and she struggled to interact with the other children in her class or participate in class activities. Both girls had attended preschool and had supportive home environments. But they nevertheless had very different challenges and strengths, and needed us as parents to encourage some things, while working to develop or instill others.

One clear example of a Mencian approach is the use of "parental inductions"—which have been shown by the psychologist Martin Hoffman to be one of the most successful forms of discipline.[15] Instead of simply reprimanding your child for doing something that hurts another child, parental inductions involve the following: calling attention to the other child's distress, having your child notice the expression on her face and her tears, and then asking your child how she would feel if someone had done the same thing to her—and how she has felt when she was hurt. This approach is very Mencian in character: it begins with the wronged party's feelings, and proceeds to your own child's feelings upon seeing the other child's distress. It seeks to draw out the child's natural sense of compassion, empathy, and concern for others, and to help her to see that other children are very much like her in their feelings and experiences. It is helpful to think here of Mencius's famous metaphor of nurturing sprouts, day in, day out, for this is one of the most readily applicable strategies a parent can employ on a daily basis. You ask your child to look into the faces of other children, to notice their tears, see that they are hurt, and think about how they would feel if they were in her shoes. You also ask your child to see another child's smile and excitement when she shares her toys, and then ask her if she feels happy when other children share with her. Parental inductions like this actively teach our children how to notice others, and to notice the ways in which we are the same. But they do this by assuming that children already have a natural sense of compassion and sympathy that can be developed.

XUNZI AND GRIT

The most important lesson Xunzi has for parents is that the process of moral cultivation will be difficult, and even painful, at times—at least if we are doing it right. He uses those harsh metaphors of steaming and bending wood and engraving metal and stone to express this. For Xunzi, the process of helping our children to develop into good people is difficult because we don't start out with the beginnings or sprouts of the virtues we need to flourish, as Mencius believed; rather, we need to *fully acquire* those traits. While Xunzi was wrong that we have to acquire *all* of the traits that we need in order to flourish and Mencius was correct that we have some good tendencies—seen in the Baby Lab experiments that highlight our innate tendency to prefer kind, helpful individuals over unkind individuals—Paul Bloom's research helps to show that Xunzi was correct that *some* of the traits we need in order to flourish will have to be acquired or instilled in us.

One of the interesting differences between Mencius and Xunzi is that while Mencius extolls qualities such as compassion and helpfulness, Xunzi focuses more on qualities like persistence and resilience. Indeed, Xunzi repeatedly emphasizes the importance of "single-mindedness"—

remaining committed to a task, and never giving up. As he puts it, "If you start carving and don't give up, then you can engrave even metal and stone."[16] The only way to acquire qualities like perseverance is through hardship, and a great deal of research has recently shown that challenge and hardship—even *failure*—is critically important for children because these qualities are essential to a flourishing life.

Perseverance, persistence, and resilience are qualities we associate with disciplined individuals, and they are a part of what the psychologist Angela Duckworth calls "grit": the ability to overcome challenges, to rise to the occasion and work hard in the face of adversity. Research has found abundant evidence that the most important aspects of our character are not fixed, and that challenges and failures serve as critical opportunities to develop some of the character traits we need to flourish. Study after study shows that perseverance and resilience in the face of challenges is a far more accurate predictor of who will complete high school or college than achievement-oriented measures such as test scores or IQ.[17]

Duckworth's research in this area has been groundbreaking. Grit, as she shows, does not correlate to IQ or SAT scores, but students at Penn who measured high on Duckworth's "Grit Scale"—a simple questionnaire that measures grit—were the students who achieved high GPAs even though they had entered college with relatively low test scores. At the National Spelling Bee, children with high grit scores were more likely to survive later rounds. And when Duckworth gave the grit test to more than twelve hundred freshman cadets at West Point as they embarked on the grueling summer training course known as Beast Barracks, the grit score turned out to be a more accurate predictor of which cadets persisted and which ones dropped out than the military's own complex evaluation (the whole candidate score).[18]

All of this confirms what Chinese philosophers believed about the importance of persistence and resilience in relation to living a fulfilling life. But there is an added, important thing to note about the difference between Mencius and Xunzi here. We naturally tend to enjoy helping others. We don't naturally enjoy persisting in difficult situations (even though we may enjoy the *results* of persisting). This is where Xunzi is correct that the task of helping our children to grow is sometimes going to be a struggle, and not just a matter of nurture or encouragement, as Mencius believed. (You might also say it is implied in Mencius's view, for one of the key character traits a farmer needs is grit.)

In such cases, Xunzi's metaphors can be highly important in reminding parents that certain kinds of growth occur not in spite of but *because of* the difficulty of the process. A child who finds writing very difficult may not be able to find the fun in practicing the strokes that form letters, no matter how many different approaches her parents and teachers try. Her hands must grow accustomed to gripping the pencil and moving it in certain ways. The process will involve repeated experiences of failure, in which the child tries to copy a letter, but is unsuccessful. This experience, however, will shape her in critical ways because she will have an opportunity to develop persistence and resilience. These are cultivated traits, and they can only be developed by experiencing and learning to respond to challenges and failures by picking oneself up and trying again. In this way, we should be grateful for our children's struggles, for the evidence tells us that they really do represent profound and necessary opportunities for growth.

But it is not as easy as it sounds. As author Paul Tough points out, "we have an acute, almost biological impulse to provide for our children, to give them everything they want and need, to protect them from dangers and discomforts both large and small. And yet we know—on some level, at least—that what kids need more than anything is a little hardship: some challenge, some deprivation that they can overcome, even if just to prove to themselves that they can. As a parent, you struggle with these thorny questions every day, and if you make the right call even half the time, you're lucky."[19] So, how can we do better? What wisdom does Xunzi have for us on this matter?

Above all, Xunzi valued self-cultivation. He believed firmly in our capacity to change. One important lesson from Xunzi is that we should not think of our children's character as fixed. Who our children are now is not who they will be for the rest of their lives. Another related Xunzian lesson is that the process of change takes a long time. The wood, metal, stone, and clay that Xunzi wrote about went through many different stages of refinement before the process of shaping was complete. Mencius' sprouts underwent a variety of stages of growth—sometimes withering and then bouncing back, other times stretching in one direction, then in another—before flourishing as mature plants. As a parent, this is terribly easy to forget, because we sometimes fear that our children will not get better, or that they are forming habits they will never outgrow, or missing opportunities that will be forever lost if they don't seize them now. This, it turns out, is seldom true.

What can we do as parents to help our children develop grit? As we have seen, Xunzi believed that the right kinds of change can happen only through hardship. And Xunzi would be keen to remind us that as parents, our posture toward failure counts for much when it comes to our children's response to it. We can't force our children to develop grit, but we can help our children look deeply at their mistakes, consider why they made them, and think about what they might have done differently. The latter, it is worth noting, involves not simply alleviating the pain of failure or avoiding it, but instead raising our comfort level with it, learning to stare it in the face and live with it. It means not avoiding the words, "You failed," or "I failed," but saying them out loud, accompanied by questions like, "How did that happen? How does it feel? Where can we go from here?" It also means sharing openly with our children about our own failures—not just past ones, but current mistakes and failures.

Another way of helping our children to develop grit

is to have realistic conversations about the people they admire, most of whom (if they are honest) have experienced profound failure. In his commencement speech at Stanford, Steve Jobs described his success in terms of three occasions of failure: when he dropped out of school (and found programming), when he lost his company (and worked to regain it), and when he discovered he had cancer and was not going to be able to beat it (and was inspired to work even harder on Apple). The great basketball player Michael Jordan describes his experience this way: "I've missed 9,000 shots in my career. I've lost almost 300 games. Twenty-six times, I've been trusted to take the game-winning shot and missed. I've failed over and over again in my life. And that is why I succeed."[20] What is especially striking is not only that Jordan remembers his failures so much that he can enumerate them—they are not simply eclipsed by his successes—but also that he does not say he succeeded *in spite of* his failures, but *because* of them. He is not just talking about his professional losses, either. In high school, Jordan didn't make the varsity basketball team until his junior year. He failed his tryout in his sophomore year and was intensely motivated to succeed by this experience of failure.

Such examples show that one of the most important things we can do as parents is work at changing the way we talk to our children about success and failure, and things that are easy and hard—and this involves changing our own way of thinking, too. Our beliefs, it turns out, matter greatly when it comes to this area. Stanford psychologist

Carol Dweck has shown that students who believe intelligence is malleable do much better than students who believe intelligence is essentially fixed and inborn, as do students who believe that their past performance is not an indication of their future results. Indeed, their mindsets predict their academic trajectories: those who believe that people can improve their intelligence actually do improve their grades.[21]

What all of this means is that our basic way of thinking about what gives us parental bragging rights should be reversed. We should take less pride in things being easy for our children, and more in their ability to work hard and persevere when things are difficult. This means that parents and children should not be ashamed of struggles and challenges in school or in any other area of a child's life; such experiences, more than experience of success or of having something come easily, will contribute to their capacity to flourish. There are a variety of ways that parents can embrace this type of approach when they are with their children. One is seen in what we praise our children for and what we proudly share with others. If we embrace this type of approach, we will focus less on, celebrate less, and talk less about (both with our children and others) achievements and outcomes of learning or practice, including test scores, grades, and skills. Instead, we will emphasize, take pride in, and help our children to take pride in how hard they are working or have worked. But here is the really difficult part: this means that we should speak with pride about *how hard something was* for our children, praising their persistence, perseverance, and resilience in the face of those challenges. And while achievements are worth celebrating—albeit always with a heavier emphasis on the hard work that got you there as opposed to the achievement itself—we will not tend to celebrate or brag about something being easy.

Parents and teachers should partner to embrace this type of approach, and a number of school systems are already working to do so through programs such as the "Growth Mindset" (rooted in Dweck's research at Stanford), which schools can adopt in order to help teachers and parents to support students in a consistent way. In our school system, parents are given a list of suggestions for implementing this approach, including the following:

○ *Talk with your child about his or her day, but guide the discussion by asking questions like: Did you make a mistake today? What did you learn? What did you do that was most difficult today?*

○ *Encourage Failure: Remind your child that each time she fails and tries again, her brain is growing stronger. Don't step in to prevent your child's failure—this is how she learns to persevere in the face of challenges.*

○ *Praise the Process: Instead of saying, "You're so smart!" praise effort, goal setting, persisting through challenges, or being creative.*

○ *Remind your child that his or her intelligence is not fixed. Remind her that when things are difficult, her brain grows if she persists through the challenge.*

○ *If your child says, "This is too hard!" help him change that to "I can't do this yet, but I will keep trying." Give him the words to say when he is feeling defeated by modeling it yourself.*[22]

While I have focused primarily on the Confucian tradition in this chapter, early Daoist philosophers would also remind us that we have an opportunity here to reconsider our basic way of thinking. We typically think of something being easy as a good thing (which is why even our children tend to brag about something being easy) and as something being hard as a bad thing. In reality, we should reverse those categories. We must stop privileging easiness over difficulty. Our basic categories are backward. The evidence suggests that there is truth in the line from the *Daodejing* that says, "Those who often think that things are easy regularly encounter difficulties. And so sages consider things difficult and in the end are without difficulties."[23]

In her book *Bird by Bird*, the author Anne Lamott tells about the time her brother procrastinated on a school project about birds. It was due the next day, "and he was at the kitchen table close to tears, surrounded by binder paper and pencils and unopened notebooks on birds, immobilized by the hugeness of the task ahead." Her father, sitting down beside him and putting his arm around her brother's shoulder, said, "Bird by bird, buddy. Just take it bird by bird."[24]

The experience of struggle, and of learning to take small steps in order to reach a goal, is so much a part of children's lives. As Xunzi put it, "If you do not accumulate little steps, you will have no way to go a thousand li." He goes on to say that even the famous horse Qi Ji—known for going a thousand miles in a single day—"could not go more than ten paces in a single leap, but with ten days of riding even an old nag can equal him, because accomplishment rests in not giving up."[25] What is fascinating here is that Xunzi does not praise Qi Ji for his extraordinary ability; rather, the accomplishment for Xunzi is not giving up. What he prizes is the possession of the virtues such as persistence and perseverance—which are, in his view, an achievement not because they lead to success as society defines it. Rather, they are virtues that enable our flourishing in a host of ways: they are necessary for moral self-cultivation—and thus for the cultivation and expression of moral virtues such as compassion, generosity, and gratitude.

꙰ 6 ꙰

The Littlest Sprout:
The Dao of Disabilities
and Challenges

Encapsulated behind an invisible but seemingly impenetrable wall. Soon he would be labeled. A tragedy. Unreachable. Bizarre. Statistically, he would fall into a category reserved for all those we see as hopeless. . . . For us the question: could we kiss the ground that others had cursed?

—BARRY KAUFMAN

If I could snap my fingers and be nonautistic, I would not—because then I wouldn't be me. Autism is part of who I am. . . . I would not want to lose my ability to think visually. I have found my place along the great continuum.

—TEMPLE GRANDIN

He looks at the way things are one and does not see what they're missing. He looks at losing a foot like shaking off dust.

—ZHUANGZI

As I played with my children at the pool, a man pushing a wheelchair caught my eye. As he made his way toward one of the pool lifts, I caught sight of the boy in the chair he pushed. It was obviously his son; you could see the resemblance. Talking to his son the whole way, he approached the lift. As I watched him gently lift his son out of his wheelchair and onto the lift, I realized that his son was not small—perhaps twelve or thirteen. And I began to think of all of the things his father had done that day, just in order to get his son to that point, from dressing him to transporting him. I thought of how frustrated I had been that day getting our three young children ready to go to the pool. Indeed, by the time we had arrived, I was exhausted and irritable. But as I watched this father, entranced, I knew that what he had done—and what he was doing now—was far more difficult. As he joined his son in the water, supporting his body entirely due to his limited mobility, he looked into his son's face, smiling, talking to him, and gently taking each arm and each leg, one by one, stretching them out and exercising them. Oblivious to the splashing and shouts of other children, he was entirely focused on his son. Ever so gently, he playfully splashed a bit of water onto his son's cheeks and forehead, eliciting a broad smile, and then a giggle. His father laughed and kissed the top of his son's head. Looking into the man's face as he returned to the task of exercising his son's arms and legs in the water, I found myself in awe of him—and not just because he had overcome so many obstacles in order to give his son this experience, but because his face bore an expression of true joy. *This is what real love looks like*, I thought. Tears sprang to my eyes. And then I looked back at my own children.

Thus far in this book, we have traced Mencius's metaphor of little sprouts, examining the ways in which they grow much in the same way our children do. Mencius also believed that we as parents have sprouts, or moral potential to be nurtured. He believed that when we witness genuine love, compassion, generosity, or gratitude in others, it stirs something within us. And when we reflect on what we have seen—not just in a way that involves thinking, but also feeling—we become better. Our natural moral tendencies—those "sprouts" of virtue within us all—grow. The combination of thinking *and* feeling are important, though, because early Chinese philosophers didn't talk about the mind and the heart separately. Rather, they believed in the "heart-mind" (*xin*, 心). Our thinking and feeling comes from the same place, and we do our best reflecting when we think *and* feel our way through a problem to a solution. And so Mencius writes, "The job of the heart-mind is to reflect. If it reflects, then it will get [Virtue]. If it does not reflect, then it will not get it."[1] Witnessing and reflecting on the virtues of others makes us better; it strengthens us, leading us to want to do better ourselves. That day at the pool, watching that father with his son, I understood what Mencius meant. It made me want to be a better mother, and it strengthened my resolve to do so. And it is an image that stays with me. Sometimes, when I find myself frustrated with my children, the image of that father flashes in my mind.

Today, more parents than ever before are aware that they are raising children with disabilities, thanks to our improved understanding of the many different kinds of learning, academic, and developmental disabilities that exist. We have learned that the Chinese philosopher Xunzi has much to say about how challenges are critical to a child's overall flourishing. What lessons do Chinese philosophers have that might help parents of children with disabilities? And how might these lessons apply to the challenges that *all* children and parents face?

ZHUANGZI'S HEROES

Although most Chinese philosophers did not often discuss people with disabilities, there is one Daoist philosopher who wrote about them extensively. While we don't know much about Zhuangzi personally, we do know he was a father—he mentions his wife and children in his writings. He doesn't talk about his childhood or early life, but he writes beautifully in classical Chinese, so we know he had the benefit of a good education. But in his writings,

Zhuangzi rejects many of his society's goals and values, criticizing those who admire only certain types of individuals as sages—including those who, like him, had the benefit of a scholarly education, and those who have gone on to hold powerful and prestigious positions in his society. Instead, he points to a variety of other examples of admirable individuals—people who, in his view, truly lead good lives, and don't just have the appearance of it. Zhuangzi's philosophical writings are especially unique because he often makes philosophical points by telling stories about vivid, memorable characters (who may or may not have been real people). In what is surely one of the most surprising themes in ancient Chinese philosophy, Zhuangzi describes individuals with different kinds of physical, intellectual, and developmental disabilities, highlighting the virtues and gifts they have because of their disabilities, rather than in spite of them.

This is a broader theme in Zhuangzi's philosophy. As philosophers Karen Carr and Philip J. Ivanhoe point out, almost everything about Zhuangzi's heroes, including their "station, occupation, appearance, and gender—make them under-appreciated, even outcasts in their society. It is, though, these very people who are able to understand and live in accordance with the Dao."[2] Zhuangzi's most famous story is about a lowly butcher who so impresses a lord with his abilities that he declares, "I have heard the words of a butcher and learned how to care for life!"[3] Zhuangzi tells stories in which woodcarvers, wheelwrights, gardeners, elderly women, hermits, and amputees instruct people in positions of power and privilege, who are grateful for their wisdom. This is why the lesson Zhuangzi offers parents in his discussion of disability is, in fact, much broader. As the philosopher Eric Schwitzgebel puts it, "Zhuangzi is challenging conventional ideas about success and failure, about what is good and what is bad, and about what skills and abilities are worth having."[4] For Zhuangzi, we have much to learn from people with disabilities—not primarily because they are proper objects of our compassion and thus can help us to become more caring people, or because they are able to succeed *in spite of* their disabilities or overcome them, but *because of* their disabilities themselves. There is a certain irony here, because on Zhuangzi's view, disabilities sometimes afford people abilities and perspectives that they would otherwise lack.

Zhuangzi is completely unflinching in his approach to disability: he never minimizes or attempts to avoid describing the disabilities of his characters. In the case of a character he calls "Splay-limb Shu," he writes that his "chin is sunk in his belly. His shoulders are above his head, pinched together so they point at the sky. His five organs are on top, his thighs tight against his ribs. . . . With splayed limbs, he is still able to keep himself alive and to live out the years Heaven gave him. What if he had splayed Virtue?"[5] Not only does Zhuangzi describe disabilities openly, but his characters with disabilities discuss their disabilities openly as well, and others openly inquire about them. Zhuangzi tells us that a passerby is startled when he sees the supreme military commander, who is missing a leg, and asks him whether he was born with his disability or whether it was caused by an injury. The commander explains that he was born that way. Partly through this openness, Zhuangzi encourages us as parents to talk openly about disabilities, to name them, and to encourage our children to name them and discuss them as they feel comfortable doing so. He is undaunted in his discussions and makes us feel as though we should be undaunted, as well. What Zhuangzi did in approaching disability this openly was deeply countercultural in his own time, when people with disabilities were devalued, disregarded, and marginalized. Ultimately, he holds up a mirror to us: How open are we about disability, even in a culture that encourages more openness than his culture did?

Another feature of Zhuangzi's stories is that his characters with disabilities are not just shown compassion or treated with respect by others, but they are also genuinely admired. He presents them as exemplars: individuals who serve as examples for others to follow. Zhuangzi introduces us to an amputee who has "as many followers as Confucius." A passerby notes, "He must be far from ordinary. Someone like that must have a special way of thinking." Indeed, the text goes on to tell us, "Death and life are big, but they make no difference to him. Heaven and earth could flip over, and it would not matter to him. . . . Looked at from their differences, liver and gall are as far apart as the states of Chu and Yue. Looked at from their sameness, the ten thousand things are all one. . . . He looks at the way things are one and does not see what they're missing."

He looks at losing a foot like shaking off dust."[6] He does not view his disability as a loss or see himself as missing something. If losing a foot is like shaking off dust, then one is in fact losing something *un*desirable—something that is a hindrance. This is related to the fact that Zhuangzi speaks directly and openly of disability. Why? Because he thinks individuals with disabilities often are able to see the world more clearly than others. They have an ability we lack.

Timothy Shriver, chairman of the Special Olympics, tells of a young athlete who was on the verge of winning first place for the first time, but when she realized her friend was behind her, she stopped and went back, put her arm around her friend, and crossed the finish line with her. Arguing along lines that resonate strongly with Zhuangzi's view, Shriver points out that in valuing first place above all else, we are following an arbitrary standard of what is praiseworthy and desirable that has been set for us by our culture and society, and which is often not good for us. Most of us will not win first place most of the time but will feel like losers, failing to appreciate the benefits of finishing the race and placing anywhere else. He argues that many people with disabilities have not uncritically conformed in the way that others have—precisely because they cannot run the same race—and that while this tends to be viewed as a shortcoming, it is more often an asset. Like Zhuangzi, Shriver believes that those with disabilities are often more in touch with how to live a good life.[7] Perhaps crossing the finish line arm in arm with a friend is, in fact, a better finish than crossing it first alone. Wouldn't we all lead happier, more fulfilled and satisfying lives if we understood that? For Zhuangzi, the answer is clear.

Our children's disabilities and challenges—as well as those of others—can help us to view the world, and our priorities, more clearly. Raun Kaufman, a therapist who works with autistic children, points out that when he asks parents of children with autism what their greatest hopes are for their children, they don't usually talk about academic achievement or earning power; rather, they dream of their children one day having a best friend, being a devoted husband or wife, and leading a happy and fulfilling life. When your child struggles with many of the things we take for granted, it can enhance your ability to see clearly what gives life meaning. As Kaufman puts it, "We need to seriously think about what is going to make our children's lives fulfilling, satisfying, rich, and meaningful to them. . . . No matter how incredible your child gets at academic subjects, it will not give her the tools she needs to relate to people, laugh at a joke, make friends and enjoy others."[8] What Kaufman notices is that most parents' deepest sensibilities tell them that the most important thing in children's lives is that they genuinely love and are loved by others; this is at the very heart of what it means to flourish as a human being. Without rich and meaningful relationships with others, we have little. But it is easy to lose sight of that, especially in a world that encourages us to seek very different goals.

KISSING THE GROUND THAT OTHERS CURSE

In addition to seeing the world and what matters more clearly, Zhuangzi's characters with disabilities also view their disabilities more clearly than we do. Much like the experiences of struggling or failing at something, we must learn to see disabilities for what they are: opportunities— and indeed, *gifts*. Zhuangzi's disabled characters have a strong sense of purpose in life, and there is a sense of purposiveness around their disability, too. When the supreme military commander explains to a passerby that he was born with his disability, he uses an ancient Chinese term that means "unique" or "special" but which also means "one-footed." He says, "Heaven makes each thing unique (*du*, 獨). But people all try to look alike."[9] The overarching point here is that we should not simply view disabilities as bad because they make us different from others. In using the term for "unique," "special," and "one-footed," Zhuangzi emphasizes that the things that make each of us unique or special are often viewed by the world as drawbacks, shortcomings, or variations of "one-footedness." But this is not how we ought to view them. Effectively, the commander says, "Heaven made me *special*. Why would I try to be like everyone else?"

Similarly, in another story, a man with a deformity similar to Shu's hobbles over to view his reflection in a well, and exclaims, "Sheesh! The maker of things really is knotting me up." But when a friend asks if he dislikes it, he responds,

> Not at all. What is there to dislike? If, in time, he turns my left arm into a rooster, I'll use it to crow the day. If he turns my right arm into a bow, I'll shoot down a dove for roasting. If he turns my buttocks into wheels and my spirit into a horse, I'll climb aboard. What better carriage? You get something when it's time. You lose it when it's passed. If you are content with the time and abide by the passing, there's no room for sorrow or joy. This is what the ancients call "loos[en] ing the bonds." If you don't loose[n] yourself, things will bind you. Nothing has ever beaten Heaven. What is there to dislike?[10]

While Zhuangzi does not explain what he means either by Heaven or "the maker of things," his characters clearly understand their disabilities as part of a grander plan or purpose, and they claim that there is nothing to dislike about them. This character goes on to describe how he can find different advantages in the various things that might go wrong with his body, emphasizing that we should be content and loosen the bonds so that things won't bind us. This line seems to reference the way in which society's standards bind us, making us unhappy when we are different from others, instead of being content and finding the good—even joy—in the way that we naturally are.

The accounts of parents of children with disabilities are a helpful resource here. The therapist Raun Kaufman, mentioned above, was once an autistic child who did not make eye contact, did not want to be touched or held, and did not talk. He performed simple, repetitive actions: spinning plates on their edges for hours on the floor, rocking back and forth, flapping his hands in front of his face. After seeking help from a variety of specialists, his parents were given little hope. As his father describes it, Raun was "encapsulated behind an invisible but seemingly impenetrable wall. Soon he would be labeled. A tragedy. Unreachable. Bizarre. Statistically, he would fall into a category reserved for all those we see as hopeless . . . unapproachable . . . irreversible. For us the question: Could we kiss the ground that others had cursed?"[11]

This is a deeply Zhuangzian question. Zhuangzi and other early Daoist philosophers believed that more often than not, we get things backward by cursing ground that should be kissed. They also believed that we tend to swim against the tide when we should swim with it. Kaufman describes how his parents attempted to swim with the tide. In an attempt to understand him and to show him love and acceptance, his mother began to join him in his repetitive behaviors: "I would sit on the floor and rock . . . and she would rock with me. I would spin a plate on its edge . . . and she would spin her own plate next to mine." Specialists worried that it would make him worse, but slowly, he began to respond to her by looking up and making eye contact. Then one day, he smiled at her. "She cherished and celebrated every look, every smile, every moment of connection for which my parents had waited so long."[12] Over the course of the next several years, Kaufman slowly improved, eventually attending mainstream public schools and then Brown University.

From a Daoist perspective, one of the keys to his parents' approach was that they did not fight their son's disability; rather, they sought to enter his world and join him. They did this in order to lead him out of that world and eventually into theirs, but they first had to learn not to attack his behavior directly. This approach embodies one of the hallmarks of the ancient Daoist tradition: that in order to address the challenges we face in life, we must learn not to fight them directly. It also embodies something we see in all of Zhuangzi's stories about people with disabilities: a refusal to flinch or to turn away from a disability. Instead, we see a willingness to embrace it, to live with it, to look deeply at it, and even to join it. Zhuangzi invites us to do precisely what Kaufman's parents did.

For Zhuangzi, there are good reasons to embrace the differences. His exemplars have keener insights as a result of their disabilities, and not in spite of them. This might strike some parents as excessively idealistic, but there are a variety of contemporary examples to consider. At age seven, the acclaimed biologist E. O. Wilson blinded himself in one eye in a fishing accident. Wishing to remain outdoors (a mark of his deep love of nature), he did not complain or seek medical treatment, and several months later, his right pupil clouded over with a cataract and the lens had to be removed. He was left with only one functional eye with a vision of 20/10, which prompted him to focus on "little things": "I noticed butterflies and ants more than other kids did, and took an interest in them automatically."[13] The loss of vision in his right eye is what led him to concentrate on insects. And that is how we got the world's leading expert on ants.

Temple Grandin is a contemporary proponent of the view that those with disabilities have unique gifts and abilities not in spite of, but by virtue of, their disabilities. Like E. O. Wilson, she is a living illustration of this. From a young age, Temple Grandin felt a deep affinity to animals, and she found that her very different (and often crippling) sensory experience of the world as an autistic person enabled her to see the world in ways that helped her understand them. Combined with her extraordinary visual spatial skills, Grandin's ability to understand the perspectives of farm animals has led her to become a leading designer of facilities and devices for handling and caring for livestock, and a passionate advocate of their humane treatment. She is a world-renowned expert on cattle psychology and behavior, and one-third of all cattle and hogs in the United States today are handled in facilities that she has designed, including humane restraint systems for both sheep and cattle as well as devices that make it possible to provide better veterinary care. Her designs have been shown to lower the animals' anxiety levels by using their natural behavior patterns, helping them to remain calm and quiet, which in turn makes them easier to manage. Grandin's cattle chutes, for instance, use curved lanes because cattle move more easily this way due to their natural circling behavior.

Grandin insists that autism contributes to her ability to appreciate how physical spaces for animals needed to be redesigned, especially her keen imagination and heightened sensory perceptions which help her to notice and understand how animals feel in various situations. (Her original title for her book *Thinking in Pictures* was *A Cow's Eye View*!) She points to a variety of similarities between the animals she works with and people with autism: cattle and sheep have supersensitive hearing, an acute sense of smell, and have "a very wide, panoramic visual field, because they are a prey species, ever wary and watchful for signs of danger. Similarly, some people with autism are like fearful animals in a world full of dangerous predators. They live in a constant state of fear, worrying about a change in routine or becoming upset if objects in their environment are moved."[14]

Grandin does not romanticize autism or downplay the tremendous challenges she faces as a result of being autistic, but at a recent lecture, she concluded by saying "If I could snap my fingers and be nonautistic, I would not— because then I wouldn't be me. Autism is part of who I am."[15] Explaining these remarks, she writes, "I would not want to lose my ability to think visually. I have found my place along the great continuum."[16] Grandin is a stunning contemporary example of a number of the things

Zhuangzi talked about—most notably his claim that some of the ways in which people with disabilities differ from us can turn out to be extraordinary abilities.

SOCIALIZATION, CONFORMITY, AND THE FREEDOM TO BE OURSELVES

Developmental and intellectual disabilities are especially interesting to consider from a Zhuangzian perspective because of his concern with socialization and conformity. For Zhuangzi, our desire and tendency to conform often makes us a danger to ourselves and others. We tend to overlook our natural and unique talents, gifts, and abilities in an attempt to become something that the world says is appealing. We are sometimes willing to restrict our diets and exercise in unhealthy ways (or even consider cosmetic surgery) out of a desire to look the way the world says we should look. But some disabilities involve a *resistance* to conformity and socialization; many individuals with developmental or intellectual disabilities have difficulty developing a sense of social awareness, including the observance of basic social conventions and a desire and tendency to conform to them. They see and respond to the world differently, and are often wholly unperturbed by being different. We can see traces of this in Temple Grandin's willingness to completely immerse herself in seeing from a cow's point of view and to embrace a line of work that follows from this ability. While many people care deeply about what their pets are thinking and feeling, most people do not care as much about cows, pigs, and sheep. Indeed, those who work closely with livestock do not enjoy the prestige (or the paychecks) of doctors or lawyers. But money and prestige shouldn't be our goals, according to Zhuangzi; he believed that pursuing these things hinders us more than it helps us. In Zhuangzi's view, thinking in ways that resist conforming to the standards of society helps to prevent certain kinds of harm, and Grandin's work is a prime example of this: her ability to see and feel from the animals' point of view has assisted veterinarians in caring for many animals, and led to a more humane form of existence for them.

There are a variety of other ways in which the lack of social awareness that is associated with autism can sometimes be good. As the mother of three children, including a son who is autistic, I have become increasingly aware of the ways in which my son's development has differed from that of his two younger sisters. Without question, his sensory experience of the world differs from ours in some of the ways that are described above, which is why he sometimes uses noise-canceling headphones. His development of social awareness, particularly with other children, was also delayed and has been more challenging than it is for most children. This has affected our family in many ways, but at times, I had the feeling that we were being spared something. For instance, his inability to participate in team sports meant that we did not spend weekends rushing from one activity to the next, as our friends did; we spent more time together as a family quietly exploring the beauty of nature in our yard and surrounding parks. And at his school, we developed exceptionally close relationships with the teachers and staff because of the countless meetings about our son's struggles—leading to friendships that enrich our lives in many ways but which never would have developed if we did not have a child with serious disabilities. There are certain benefits that we have experienced as a result of being unable to do some of the things other families do, and these are having a lasting (and positive) impact on all of us.

Zhuangzi would urge us to notice several things here. First, it is simply more constructive to embrace the reality of the situation and take a "What's not to like?" sort of attitude, as Zhuangzi's characters do. Now, that is not to say that I would not eliminate my son's autism if I could. But I suspect that Zhuangzi would find such hypothetical mental exercises to be of little value, for that is not the life we have been given. Despite the fact that I sometimes wish our son could play sports with other children, it is not particularly productive or good for us to bemoan the fact that our son cannot be in loud, crowded settings or observe the rules of a game like other children. And it is not realistic to think that trying to force him to do so will serve as the therapy that will lead him there. *How we see our children's challenges and their effect on our lives matter a lot as parents.* This dimension of Zhuangzi's thought is remarkably pragmatic and clear-eyed, and it is also therapeutic: it is good for us because it encourages us to stop trying to swim upstream against a current that is too powerful to overcome.

Zhuangzi offers a broader lesson here that goes beyond disability. He believes that it is *better* for us to resist conforming to society's norms and expectations in favor of following our nature (and in favor of being *in* nature, too). This is a lesson that everyone can learn from: from Zhuangzi's perspective, we can all benefit from paying a little less attention to what everyone else is doing and more attention to our natural gifts and the things that bring us joy. I once had a friend tell me that she envied the way that we spent our weekends because her son really did not enjoy playing sports and she found all of the practices and games exhausting. But she felt enormous pressure to conform to what everyone else was doing; she worried that her son would be a social outcast if he did not participate in the same activities as other children. I was taken aback by her perspective—that our son's disability freed us from what, to her, felt like social pressure to conform. Zhuangzi would find her worries about her son being a social outcast particularly interesting.

These remarks resonate with Raun Kaufman's emphasis on the goal of wanting our children to have real friendships. While Zhuangzi lifts up social outcasts as exemplars, as we have seen, his characters are certainly not isolated or friendless, but he might point out the need to be open to different friendships. Our son's disabilities have led to some different relationships (for him and for us) than the soccer-field friendships that we might have if he were not autistic. In addition to the friendships we have developed with his teachers and their families, one of the benefits that comes from our son's participation in special education is that his friends include other children with a wide range of disabilities. More than anything else, these relationships lead me to say, with Temple Grandin, that if I could snap my fingers and make our son nonautistic, something valuable would be lost.

In the documentary *The Address*, by Ken Burns, which follows students at a private school for children with disabilities, the director of the school describes a conversation he once had with the parents of one of the students. They told him they just wanted their son to be normal. And he replied, "His job isn't to be normal, but to be himself."[17] The point here is one worth savoring: in order for us to flourish, we have to be ourselves. It is very difficult to lead a happy, satisfying, fulfilled life if we are trying to be—or to become—someone else. And we tend to miss out on realizing the unique potential in each of us. The school director pinpointed the fact that "normal" indicated conformity—being like everyone else. Flourishing, though, is an individual matter. We don't flourish in the same way, or on the same paths. This is something we see clearly with Temple Grandin and in Zhuangzi's characters with disabilities, and it is something Zhuangzi took seriously: in order to flourish, we must find our own path. We must be ourselves.

I want to offer one final illustration of how autistic challenges relating to social awareness suggest that Zhuangzi was on the right track. Our son attended a preschool program for children with special needs in one of the most diverse elementary schools in the United States. (We live in a diverse area, so he and his sisters have always spent time around children of many different races and ethnicities.) When his younger sister, at age three, began to ask questions about the different skin colors of her friends, I suddenly realized that our son had never asked those questions, despite the fact that he was highly verbal and very observant. To the contrary, I began to realize that he did not seem to see—or perceive—differences in skin color. He did not see difference where others did; he saw only people. I began to pay attention to this, and it took several years before he began to ask the questions his sister had asked (and which other boys in his class had asked) much earlier. This would be included on a long list of "developmental delays" noted by specialists, and it was a delay that fell neatly into the category of social awareness— challenges relating to how one perceives and interacts with one's peers, which are characteristic of children on the autism spectrum. But what intrigued me was that it was an *asset* that he was unaware of racial and ethnic differences for much longer than other children; he interacted with children and adults of all races and ethnicities in exactly the same way. And on the day that he finally asked me about differences in skin color—years later than his sister—I felt that something had been lost. Today, our son and daughter both have close friends of different races and ethnicities; I do not think there are enduring ramifications of this developmental difference. I do, though, think that this is a good example of what it means to talk about natural goodness and the way being socialized can have a corrupting influence on it.

A final noteworthy feature of Zhuangzi's disabled characters is that they are freer than the rest of us to live a good life. They are unencumbered by many of the false ideals that are foisted on us by our culture and society. As a result, it is easier for them to lead good, simple lives. Consider the case of Splay-limb Shu: "Mending clothes and taking in laundry he makes enough to fill his mouth. Winnowing leftover grain he gets enough to feed ten people. When the people in charge are calling out troops, Splay-limb wanders among them waving goodbye. When they are press-ganging workers he is exempted as a chronic invalid. When they dole out grain to the sick, he gets three measures, and ten bundles of firewood. With splayed limbs, he is still able to keep himself alive and to live out the years Heaven gave him."[18] Shu does not become a wealthy king or a decorated soldier, but his needs are met, and he does not die young. His life is simple, but Zhuangzi lauds a simple, contented manner as a worthwhile goal. In another story, Zhuangzi's friend complains about a big tree that is completely useless: "Its trunk is so gnarled it won't take a chalk line, and its branches are so twisted they won't fit a compass or square. It stands by the road but no builder looks twice at it." Zhuangzi responds, "You have a big tree and are upset that you can't use it." Then he asks him why he doesn't just nap beneath it in the shade. "It won't fall to

any axe's chop and nothing will harm it. Since it isn't any
use, what bad can happen to it?"[19]

Here, Zhuangzi offers parents a profound opportunity
to reflect on the goals we have for our children by raising
a broader question about conformity, and our uncritical
acceptance of the standards of our culture and society.
One of the most important features of the stories Zhuangzi
tells about those with disabilities is the way he tells them:
directly and resolutely. In doing so, Zhuangzi conveys the
message that we should not flinch, speak in hushed voices,
or be ashamed of disabilities or other differences. This is
not just a message that people in ancient China needed to
hear. Even in a modern society where individuality and
creativity are highly valued, we still have a high degree
of conformity. It never felt "okay" that my child behaved
differently, played differently, and responded differently
than other children, and this has often made it tempting
to try to create the appearance that he is just like others—
usually with mixed or little success. In some neighbor-
hoods, if you have a child who is unable to participate in
team sports, you may very well have the only child on the
block who doesn't play soccer. And people will find it odd
when you do not do what everyone else does. This has not
changed since Zhuangzi's time.

Yet Zhuangzi urges us to be unashamed for multiple reasons. He believes that those with disabilities have
unique and special insights to bring, including an understanding of themselves and the world that is often clearer
than the view the rest of us have. But Zhuangzi aims to

not only appreciate, accept, and admire those who are disabled, but also to help all of us view ourselves differently and live differently as a result. For Zhuangzi, by looking to those with disabilities, we can all be made to examine whether we are trying to conform to some artificial standard that has been imposed on us, or whether we are finding joy in who, what, and where we are.

✣ 7 ✣

From Sprout to Plant:
The Dao of Vocation

Thread, in the hands of a loving mother,
Becomes the coat to be worn by her wandering son.
As the time draws near for his departure, she stitches it tightly,
Fearing that he may be slow to return.
Who would ever claim that a tender blade of grass
Could ever repay the warmth of three spring seasons?
—MENG JIAO, "WANDERING SON"

n the children's book *Miss Rumphius*, a little girl sits on her great-aunt's knee and, listening to her stories of faraway places, declares that she, too, will grow up and travel the world.

> *"That is all very well, little Alice," says my aunt, "but there is a third thing you must do."*
> *"What is that?" I ask.*
> *"You must do something to make the world more beautiful."*
> *"All right," I say.*
> *But I do not know yet what that can be.*[1]

It is a striking piece of advice, isn't it? But this is at least partly because of what her great-aunt does *not* say. She does not advise her to *make the world a better place*. She also does not tell her that she should be successful. She tells her to do something to make the world more beautiful. And aren't there many different things that enrich our lives, making them more beautiful and bringing us meaning, fulfillment, and happiness? Much of this book has centered on ancient Chinese critiques of the pursuit of wealth, prestige, and power. But if earning power and prestigious schools and employers are not our goals for our children, how should we guide them when it comes to developing their interests, abilities, and talents?

DISCOVERING YOUR CHILD'S VOCATION: LESSONS FROM ZHUANGZI

The early Daoist philosopher Zhuangzi believed that the most admirable people in the world are those who have found their true vocation—something that they are not only excellent at doing, but also something that they find genuine fulfillment and joy in doing. He was so deeply interested in what these people are like and how they come to flourish in such remarkable ways that he wrote far more about the topic of vocation than any other Chinese philosopher. As we saw in the previous chapter, Zhuangzi's philosophical writings are unique because he often used stories—as opposed to explicit arguments—to make his points. As a result, his work is especially incisive when it comes to exploring what a life well lived looks like. The colorful characters in his stories make a variety of contributions—they make the world a little better, but they also make the world more beautiful.

Zhuangzi's view aligns with the goals that most of us have for our children in both obvious and less obvious ways: we all hope that our children will find something they are good at, and we also hope they will find something they enjoy doing. But Zhuangzi also challenges widespread views in a couple of important ways: First, while it is clear that the individuals Zhuangzi describes are appreciated and even admired by others and truly excellent at what they do, he never declares that they are the best or gives us a sense of how they "rank" relative to others. They are certainly not famous. Rather, what is important is that they have found their place in the world—a place where they truly feel at home and can use their unique gifts and abilities. The philosopher Philip J. Ivanhoe calls this metaphysical comfort or oneness with the world.[2] Second, Zhuangzi strongly emphasizes the overall sense of satisfaction and flourishing that individuals have in relation to their vocation, but this does not come from external rewards such as the recognition of others or a high salary; rather, it comes from taking joy in *what they do*. Finally, he thoroughly disregards the matters of money, prestige, and power in relation to vocation. Zhuangzi's exemplars include cooks and butchers, wheelwrights and woodcarvers. They do not include anyone who enjoys fame or prestige, has a lot of power, or earns a lot of money for what they do. There are no political leaders, government officials, or even scholars. His views are bound up with his own autobiography. He is an excellent writer, so we know Zhuangzi benefited from an education, but he left his privileged roots behind, opting for a simpler, quieter life. He declines political positions. He writes that he is poor but that he has the Way, so it doesn't matter. His stories help to explain why.

Among Zhuangzi's most well-known characters is a butcher who "was cutting up an ox for Lord Wenhui.

Wherever his hand touched, wherever his shoulder leaned, wherever his foot stepped, wherever his knee pushed—with a zip! With a whoosh!—he handled his chopper with aplomb, and never skipped a beat." The passage goes on to compare his movements to a dance, and Lord Wenhui admires him, exclaiming, "Ah, excellent, that technique can reach such heights!"[3]

Zhuangzi's choice of a butcher is not incidental. Zhuangzi believed that individuals who buy into society's false goals would never be able to align their lives with the Dao and flourish. These people are typically unable to find the path that will make them the happiest and the most fulfilled because the goals of wealth, prestige, and power are so seductive that they actually blind us to our deepest intuitions, preventing us from being able to see clearly enough to find the Way. Even Zhuangzi's exemplars find this to be a challenge, and find that they have to work at removing themselves from the world in order to do their work. A woodcarver who carves beautiful bell stands says, "When I am going to make a bell stand . . . I always fast in order to still my mind. When I have fasted for three days, I no longer have any thought of congratulations or rewards, of titles or stipends. When I have fasted for five days, I no longer have any thought of praise or blame, of skill or clumsiness. . . . My skill is concentrated and all outside distractions fade away."[4]

Note that Zhuangzi's bell stand carver must work to dismiss the distracting thoughts of rewards, titles, or stipends. These are not the proper goals to have—in

Zhuangzi's view, money, wealth, and prestige are obstacles to our flourishing, not paths to it. They are things to be avoided, not pursued. And so Zhuangzi says, "Don't make a name for yourself or follow a plan. Don't take responsibility or claim knowledge. Thoroughly embody what can't be exhausted and wander where you can't be seen."[5] In order to find our true vocation and embrace it, we must learn to turn away from the world's goals and values and instead accord with something larger than ourselves. This is certainly what we can take away from the bell stand carver's story.

But even if we can understand not pursuing fame or prestige, why not follow a plan? Well, Zhuangzi had a couple of concerns about plans. For one, our plans tend to have fixed goals, and fixed paths to get us to those goals. In his view, one of the best things we can do as parents is allow our children the opportunity to explore. This means not only that we should refrain from telling them what they should be, but it also means that we should stop trying to get our children to focus on a particular path while they are still children. There are, of course, a host of ways in which this happens as they grow. Some high schools require students to declare "tracks." Colleges require students to declare majors at a certain point, but even before then, too many students feel that they ought to go to college knowing what their path will be—partly because they believe this type of tight focus is what college admissions boards want. The world of children's activities sometimes seems oriented toward helping parents to determine what their child's "thing" is—as if there is only one "thing" and as if we could determine it now—and as if that is helpful or even necessary for success. Zhuangzi rejects all of this, and he urges us to stop and examine how we might be undermining our children's ability to explore and grow as people. You see, Zhuangzi contends that exploration is not a means to an end, but an end worth pursuing in itself.

The tendency to see exploration as a means to an end (specifically a means to the end of helping your child find the thing they are good at) in many cases stems from our worry that the only way our children will truly become good at something is if they start young. While it is true that *some* people start cultivating a particular talent or skill at a very young age and that turns out to be their vocation, in most cases, that's not what happens. Acclaimed musicians do not even follow the same path in this regard. Wynton Marsalis picked up the trumpet for the first time at age fourteen—not when he was three. Zhuangzi strongly emphasizes the diversity of paths, and the very different ways that those paths unfold. There are particularly important lessons for us as parents here with respect to our children's struggles. Acclaimed children's author Beverly Cleary struggled with reading in first grade, despite having plenty of support (her mother was a teacher). As she describes it, "The first grade was separated into three reading groups—Bluebirds, Redbirds, and Blackbirds. I was a Blackbird. To be a Blackbird was to be disgraced. I wanted to read, but somehow could not."[6] By third grade, though, she caught up and started to spend a lot of time reading and at the library. By sixth grade, Cleary's reading and writing had improved so much that one of her teachers suggested that she become a children's writer.

Zhuangzi's butcher and woodcarver, as well as contemporary examples like Marsalis and Cleary, remind us of how important stories are for us and for our children. They speak volumes. (As my own daughter struggled with reading, thinking of Beverly Cleary's story reminded me that this is a long and unpredictable journey—more than any adage ever could.) Indeed, one of the most important things we find in Zhuangzi's writings are stories of real people: people with disabilities, people who faced challenges and made mistakes, and people who know how to be themselves—who realize their own potential and find joy in their unique constellation of relationships and abilities. In describing people who found their true vocation, Zhuangzi does not privilege particular professions or paths over others. He sees that as a part of the illness of conformity that we contract from our culture and society.

Zhuangzi also intentionally points to ordinary people—not just famous people—who are leading good lives, and who are doing work that is fulfilling, satisfying, and at which they are very good. Indeed, Zhuangzi's exemplars are appealing because they are excellent at what they do. But although others admire and appreciate what they do, none of them are famous, rich, or powerful. Indeed, in holding up such individuals for us to admire, Zhuangzi is urging us to open our eyes and look around. As the later Chinese philosopher Wang Yangming put it, "The people filling the streets are sages!" What about the teacher who has a knack for helping struggling first-graders learn to read (and to find it fun)? What about the builder who knows exactly what needs to be fixed (and what does not need to be fixed) on a house, after looking at it for just a few minutes? The chances that they will ever be recognized with an award are very small, even if they are outstanding at what they do. But the chances that others will notice them are very high. For Zhuangzi, the sages most worthy of our admiration are precisely those we find in positions that lack prestige, power, or hefty earning power. Zhuangzi knows that having such things is not simply a direct result of excellence or merit. He also believes that society tends to recognize a lot of the wrong individuals because it has the wrong goals.

It is equally important to note that Zhuangzi's exemplars display abilities that are not simply a matter of "native talent" or "genius" that required no cultivation. After Lord Wenhui compliments the butcher, he sheathes his knife and says, "When I first began cutting up oxen, I did not see anything but oxen. Three years later, I couldn't see the whole ox. And now, I encounter them with spirit and don't look with my eyes. . . . That's why after nineteen years the blade of my chopper is still as though fresh from the grindstone." In all of his stories of individuals who have found their true vocation, Zhuangzi explicitly notes that they cultivated and refined their abilities for years in order to achieve the kind of mastery they exhibit. The butcher did not simply pick up a knife and immediately show evidence that it was "his thing." In one story, a wheelwright says he has been working for seventy years at his craft, describing the refinement of his abilities that it has required: "When I chisel a wheel, if I hit too softly, it slips and won't bite. If I hit too hard, it jams and won't move. Neither too soft nor too hard—I get it in my hand and respond with my mind. But my mouth cannot put it into words. There is an art to it. But your servant can't show it to his own son, and he can't get it from me. I've done it this way seventy years and am growing old chiseling wheels."[7]

Zhuangzi's butcher says something similar: "I rely on the Heavenly patterns, strike in the big gaps, am guided by the large fissures, and follow what is inherently so. I never touch a ligament or tendon, much less do any heavy wrenching!" But that is not to say the work is easy. Indeed, like the wheelwright, in the butcher's case part of what makes his work enjoyable is the focus that it sometimes requires, despite his mastery of it: ". . . when I get to a hard place, I see the difficulty and take breathless care. My gaze settles! My movements slow!" Indeed, part of the joy is that the butcher and the wheelwright use their minds—it takes great intelligence to do this work. We see something similar in the woodcarver who makes bell stands, when he describes what he does after he stops thinking about worldly goals like rewards or stipends: "After that, I go into the mountain forest and examine the Heavenly nature of the trees. If I find one of superlative form, and I can see a bell stand there, I put my hand to the job of carving; if not, I let it go. This way I am simply matching up

'Heaven' with 'Heaven.'" When he looks at the trees, he sees something that the rest of us do not see.

This is reminiscent of that twisted tree Zhuangzi describes. It stands by the roadside, and no builder looks twice at it. Deemed useless, it is able to live out its years under Heaven because it doesn't fall to any axe's chop. For Zhuangzi, one of the reasons why the butcher, wood-carver, and wheelwright are models of what we should hope for in our children is that they are unfettered by worldly goals such as wealth and fame—goals that harm us, cut us down, and leave us empty and unfulfilled no matter how much we achieve. Zhuangzi's artisans are able to take joy in their work partly because these things are not of concern to them. But they also choose to embrace something that the world passed by. They are in the world but not of it.

There is something deeply spiritual about Zhuangzi's account of these individuals. This makes it seem more like they have found vocations than jobs. We see this in the woodcarver's remarks about matching up Heaven with Heaven. He means that each thing has something it is meant to become—a nature or destiny that represents its true purpose, and the fulfillment of its destiny. But in saying he matches a tree up with what it is meant to become—a bell stand or something else entirely—he also emphasizes that he does not ordain or decide that purpose. And his concluding remark is telling: "That's probably the reason that people wonder if the results were not made by spirits." Since he is "matching up 'Heaven' with 'Heaven'" in his work—following the plan that is ordained by something much larger than himself and yet still a mystery—it appears divinely inspired. This gives new meaning to what the word "exceptional" can denote.

Along these same lines, Zhuangzi's butcher says to Lord Wenhui, "What I value is the Way, which goes beyond technique . . . I encounter them with spirit and don't look with my eyes. Sensible knowledge stops and spiritual desires proceed. . . . There are spaces between those joints, and the edge of the blade has no thickness. If you use what has no thickness to go where there is space—oh! There's plenty of extra room to play about in." Lord Wenhui replies, "Excellent! I have heard the words of a butcher and learned how to care for life!" All of this suggests that much more is going on here than work. The butcher takes joy in his work, and even finds spiritual fulfillment in it. It is about the Way, "which goes beyond technique." When we find our true vocation, we find a deeply spiritual form of fulfillment. And here it is important to note that for Zhuangzi, we are deeply spiritual beings. We are more than simply bodies capable of mastering skills, and minds capable of great feats. Zhuangzi is after a deeper level of fulfillment for us. He urges us to seek more, to be more.

VOCATION, CHARACTER, AND INTELLIGENCE

As a parent, it is tempting to want your child to find "their thing" so that they can win prestige. At a certain level, nothing is more natural for us as parents than to desire the world to celebrate and appreciate our children just as we do. We think they are wonderful—we recognize their unique gifts, not only because we spend a lot of time with them, but also because we love them. I remember one of my mentors telling me that when his own children started college, he thought, "I wonder if their professors know what special people they are?" And then it occurred to him: every one of his students had parents who felt the same way. But we must recognize that few if any people will ever love and appreciate our children the way we do. From a Confucian perspective, that is not something to bemoan, but to celebrate. One of the great gifts of parenting is that we get to witness, up close, in the most intimate way, the miracle of a human life. This ought to lead us to view all children differently—and for most of us, I think it does—even if we aren't fully aware of it. After having our first child, I discovered that when I went to work the next fall, I was no longer able to watch parents helping their children move into the dorms for their freshman year without getting emotional. I had understood, intellectually, what these parents were doing before, but now I saw it—and felt it—as a parent. And my perspective was never the same.

When it comes to the desire for prestige—seen very clearly in the desire for our children to be exceptional or to be the best at something—it is also important to dig a little deeper. This is what Michael Roth is trying to get us to do when he points out that by encouraging our children to apply to colleges or employers that turn away the greatest number of qualified applicants, we are teaching them to value things only to the extent that other people are deprived of them.[8] We tend to blindly accept that certain schools are "prestigious" and that aiming to go to them is a worthy goal. In wanting our children to be the best at something, we are embracing the same type of view. Wanting your child to be very good at what they do looks quite different from this, just as wanting your child to go to a good college looks quite different from wanting your child to go to an Ivy League school. And while we are examining uncomfortable hidden views and assumptions, it is worth looking at the desire for prestige and recognition that we have as parents, as well. We invest so much in our children, and we want to see the fruits of our efforts.

At the same time, we are, at particular points, reminded of the truth: that, as the Lebanese American writer Kahlil Gibran so poignantly puts it, "Your children are not your children." Much of who our children are is not a result of our efforts, our decisions, or who we are. That can be very difficult—sometimes even excruciating—to accept. The most important way in which my son's disability made me a better parent is that it helped me to embrace the fact that my children's paths will not be the same as my path, and that there is much about their path that I do not get to control. Even though I never thought of having my children follow the same career path as I did, it was hard to grapple with the fact that their path might be very different from mine. In the early days of our son's diagnosis, I remember telling a friend, "This just isn't the journey we expected to be on as parents." He wisely replied, "No one gets to take that journey." For Zhuangzi, if we are able to be open to our children becoming something that is very different from ourselves or what we originally envisioned for them, it can be a marvelous gift—not just to them, but also to us.

Yet Zhuangzi does not look at this picture with rose-colored glasses, and despite his rejection of wealth, prestige, and power, it is very important to notice what his exemplars are not. To begin, they are not mediocre at what they do; rather, they are all excellent—and in some cases they are excellent at things we never even dreamed someone could be excellent at. They are also not unrecognized by others. To the contrary, the butcher, the wheelwright, and the woodcarver are *all* admired by others—and sometimes by people in very high stations (a lord, a duke, and a marquis, respectively). All of these admirers express the wish that they could lead such remarkable lives and be as good at what they do. Another noteworthy feature of his exemplars is that they are all earning a living quite successfully. They are not beggars. They all work for a living. They all contribute to their society. But notice the incredible diversity of their contributions: they are meeting people's needs, but not in a grandiose way. Everyone needs meat cut, wheels crafted, and wood carved for various purposes. It is also clear that Zhuangzi acknowledges a variety of needs—and among those is certainly the need for beauty, seen in the woodcarver's bell stands.

What is most remarkable, though—and what is most important—is that each of these individuals find meaning and joy in these everyday forms of work. And their fulfillment, joy, and mastery of what they do overflow so much that it is practically contagious. Those watching them don't simply say, "That's a good butcher." They say, "I've learned how to care for life." Zhuangzi describes individuals who have truly found their place in the world, and this is precisely what the onlookers marvel at.

Yet when people marvel at the woodcarver's work and he is asked, "What art is it you have?" he replies, "I am only a craftsman—how would I have any art?" None of Zhuangzi's exemplars view themselves or their contributions as being more important or better than those of others. One of the main undercurrents in Zhuangzi's philosophy is the rich diversity of good lives, and the importance of finding your place in the world. Those who understand the Dao and who lead good lives also recognize how exceptional diverse kinds of people doing different kinds of work are. And so, despite how remarkable they are, nowhere in Zhuangzi's writings do we find individuals who desire to hold positions that exclude the largest number of people, or to stand out from the crowd.

Among his insights concerning these individuals is that they are highly reflective and articulate. Zhuangzi highlights their intelligence, but they are not academic overachievers. What we can learn as parents from Zhuangzi is to broaden our understanding of intelligence and, as a result, our appreciation for the remarkable diversity of aptitudes, abilities, and skills. This raises an important question: What, exactly, do we think intelligence is? I was amazed when my first-grader came home one day and told me that she was not as smart as her classmates. Alarmed, I asked why, and she answered that she was not as good at math. She equated intelligence with mastery of particular skills. And her thinking was not that far from widespread views in our culture concerning intelligence and cognitive skills. Why do we tend to associate intelligence with cognitive skills such as knowing how to work certain types of math problems or decode words, as opposed to skills in other areas? All of these skills are acquired; they all must be taught. With academic skills such as reading, the earliest readers do not consistently turn out to be the strongest readers later. And although IQ tests, as well as standardized tests such as the ACT and SAT, measure certain cognitive skills (such as the ability to calculate and to recognize letters and words), we know that children's scores on these tests are relatively easy to change and do not predict who will complete or even do well in college or succeed in other areas. As Paul Tough bluntly puts it, what matters most in a child's development "is not how much information we can stuff into her brain in the first few years. What matters, instead, is whether we are able to help her develop a very different set of qualities, a list that includes persistence, self-control, curiosity, conscientiousness, grit, and self-confidence. Economists refer to these as noncognitive skills, psychologists call them personality traits, and the rest of us sometimes think of them as character."[9]

Why don't we value other skill types as highly? Why don't we regard them as indicators of intelligence, or equate them with intelligence? There is a cultural history here that is worth reflecting on. The skills that we widely equate with intelligence (e.g., in math and reading) at one time were solely the skills of the wealthy and privileged. The skills that we do not equate with intelligence—and that we quickly call "skills" rather than smarts—are those traditionally belonging to non-elites, like carpenters and butchers. Elites regarded their own skills as indicators of intelligence and the skills of others as nothing more than skills.

Isn't it astonishing that, as far as we may have come as a culture and as much as we work toward and prize genuine equality, we automatically retain so much of our cultural heritage? The tendency to value the scholarly skills of elites and devalue the vocational skills of others is not confined to one culture, though. It was very much a part of Zhuangzi's culture, which was why he argued vehemently against valuing the abilities and work of scholars over others. He criticized Confucian philosophers for overvaluing scholarly abilities—over time, East Asian cultures did come to value academic achievement greatly, partly as a result of Confucianism. But there is a notable difference between modern Chinese culture and the views of ancient Confucian philosophers on this point. Although ancient Confucians did believe that we should help our children to be learned, this didn't mean they should be academic overachievers. The knowledge they sought was meant to make them wiser and better able to serve the world. And as we saw earlier in this work, ancient Confucians stressed developing a love of learning over how much you know. So although Zhuangzi is correct that Confucians emphasize learning more than he and other early Daoist thinkers did, it is important to remember that the contemporary emphasis on academic achievement in some East Asian cultures is a far cry from the ancient Confucian emphasis on learning.

Harvard professor Howard Gardner developed his influential theory of multiple intelligences in the early 1980s, arguing that the traditional notion of intelligence, based on IQ testing, was far too limited. He eventually proposed eight types of intelligences to account for the broad range of potential in children and adults, including spatial intelligence, bodily-kinesthetic intelligence, musical intelligence, and naturalistic intelligence.[10] Another example is seen in the now-widespread acknowledgment of something called "social intelligence": the ability to build and navigate social relationships well—something that, without question, requires tremendous intelligence. But it is also something that some of the "greatest minds" in history—that is, those we regard as having outstanding cognitive skills in areas like mathematics—clearly lacked.

On the other hand, Zhuangzi urges us not to privilege intelligence over other traits, or to label every ability that impresses us as a form of intelligence (simply because we uncritically attach more value to intelligence than virtues like kindness or the mad variety of skills and talents people can have). Instead, his stories encourage us to value the abilities of people who can work with their hands, be they quilters, potters, woodworkers, bakers, or butchers, *and* to value the intelligence it takes to do these kinds of work. Zhuangzi's skilled exemplars are certainly intelligent, but that is not all that he is trying to get us to see. He wants us to value a butcher's skills as much as we value the skills of successful business leaders or politicians. In his view, we should not prefer that our child become one over the other. Many parents do this, desiring wealth and prestige. He—along with all of the Chinese philosophers I have discussed in this book—would also be keen to point out that wealth, prestige, and power are not sources of flourishing for our children or for us. They do not deny the importance of making a living, and being able to provide for oneself and one's family—as we have seen, all of Zhuangzi's exemplars do that. But for all of these philosophers, the real question—for all of us—ought to be what brings us genuine joy, satisfaction, and fulfillment, a sense that we have found our place in the world and are at home in it, and that we are making our corner of the world a little kinder, a little gentler, and a more beautiful place to be.

And we should celebrate, rather than decry, the fact that each of us is inclined differently, with a different combination of gifts and abilities. There is much to celebrate in a child who can get along with every member of his class, even as he struggles academically. For Zhuangzi this does not mean we should simply regard him as having high "social intelligence" and view this as predicting his future. Zhuangzi insists that a child's future is not fixed, nor is it easy to predict. As parents, we must do all we can to help our children to develop in as many areas as possible, knowing that what we see in them at age six may or may not be the same as what their strengths will be at age twenty. Of all the lessons Chinese philosophers have to teach us, perhaps this is the most important: what our children are now is not the same as what they can and will become.

Zhuangzi would want us, even as we work to cultivate our child's strengths and weaknesses—putting our hands into the soil day in and day out as we tend those little sprouts—to acknowledge, affirm, take pride in, and value the strengths our children have, especially those skills, abilities, and aptitudes that are outside the scope of what our culture celebrates. Here, Zhuangzi contends that the task of parenting can be incredibly countercultural—at least if we do it well.

There is something deeply American about the view that we ought to celebrate and embrace our diversity, and learn to genuinely appreciate the different lives, paths, and gifts of others. Those who admire Zhuangzi's exemplars are admirable, too, because they recognize and value the diverse vocations of others. Zhuangzi, then, would caution us against the hidden elitism of advocating a college education for all; in his view, this looks too much like we are encouraging conformity and incapable of appreciating the meaning and value in work that does not require higher education.

BIODIVERSITY AND LITTLE SPROUTS

What are some of the ways we might do better, both as individual parents and as a society, to value diverse vocations? To begin, we will need to work at not privileging particular professions over others. Becoming an elementary school teacher or a nurse should not be any less desirable than becoming a doctor, a lawyer, a businessperson, or an engineer. Teaching and nursing are also excellent examples of undervalued professions, at least partly if not primarily because more women traditionally held them than men. As a result, these roles are associated with women and thus undervalued just as women have been.

Additionally, Zhuangzi serves as an important resource for us because we must think about the paths to the professions he describes. How does one become a butcher or a carpenter if it is not part of one's family business or trade? This requires us to consider the lack of trade schools and alternative educational opportunities, and the excess of college-educated individuals. And these are questions well worth considering, in light of the daunting cost of a college education. But we will also have to push ourselves to continue to consider, and reconsider, our cultural history. In this nation of immigrants, many of us have worked toward the goal of getting a college education—something that was not an option for many of our grandparents or even our parents. We tend to view the onward march of progress generationally: our expectation is that our children will go to college in order to have a better life. Here is where Zhuangzi cautions us to be careful. We should not assume that a better life for our children necessarily involves a particular range of careers, or even a college education. A college education should be accessible to all, but so too should a variety of other educational paths— paths that would, for instance, allow one to become a highly skilled carpenter, cook, or butcher. And we should readily acknowledge, as Zhuangzi does, that being excellent in these professions requires many years of learning, working hard, and intelligence.

In parenting, embracing such a view involves a different way of being with our children. Just as Zhuangzi helps us to look deeply at the lives of butchers, wheelwrights, and woodcarvers, we must help our children to look deeply at the diverse good lives of those around them. We can help them to notice, appreciate, respect, marvel at, and express gratitude for the many kinds of work that others do as a way of teaching them to value the rich variety of vocations that others have—and that they might one day have, too.

Zhuangzi's stories come from ancient China, but we are surrounded by similar examples. *Washington Post* columnist Petula Dvorak points out, "In a culture relentless in its obsession with college and upward mobility, those with gifts and talents outside the curriculum are undervalued. The people who actually make the world function with

hands, backs and brains get little in the way of direction."
Her brother, she says, "was one of those guys. Since he
was tiny, he loved to fish. But my family—and me, too—
pushed him to do something more mainstream." But after
years of trying to make his way through college and working different jobs, "I saw it, they saw it, he saw it. He was
miserable." And he began to pursue jobs that would allow
him to fish: the tackle store, guiding, working on a salmon
crew, eventually owning his own boat and fishing com-
mercially. As his sister put it, "He found it. Without the
classes we tried to cram him into, without the manage-
ment track, the union rules, the human resources paper-
work, the timecards. . . . He found it on his own, a way to
live his passion in full."[11]

His story is reminiscent of one of Zhuangzi's. While
Zhuangzi was angling by the Pu River, the king of Chu
sent two officials to him, asking if he would serve as an
administrator in their kingdom. Without looking up from
his fishing pole, Zhuangzi said, "I've heard Chu has a sacred
turtle. It's been dead three thousand years and the king
keeps it wrapped and boxed and stored up in his ancestral
hall. Now, would that turtle rather have its bones treasured in death, or be alive dragging its tail in the mud?"
The two officials replied, "It would rather be alive dragging its tail in the mud." And Zhuangzi said, "Go! I'll keep
my tail in the mud, too." In rejecting the offer of a powerful, prestigious position, Zhuangzi gives his reasoning: to
be treasured and celebrated in that position would be like
being treasured and celebrated in death. He chooses what

he loves to do over the position the world would celebrate. And so he chooses life.

One of the core lessons Zhuangzi teaches us is that leading a flourishing life does not just involve skill mastery, intelligence, or achievement, but finding something that allows us to dance in time to the rhythms of the Dao. While Confucians believed we gain the ability to do this as we develop virtues, Zhuangzi adds to this picture the role that finding our true vocation can play in a good life. For Zhuangzi, the question is not only how our sprouts are nourished by the sun, rain, and other forces, but also what we will grow into. He emphasizes diversity, from barley sprouts to the sprouts of weeping willows, pines, and poplars—from straight trees to twisted trees, and everything in between.

And so we end the way we began: with the image of those little sprouts growing in a field. Through their metaphors, Chinese philosophers speak to us in a universal language. And so the first time I read Mencius's philosophy and his metaphor of sprouts, it felt deeply familiar. Growing up in an Irish American home, the thickly brogued singing voices of Tommy Makem and Liam Clancy often played on our stereo. Of all the songs on their records, my brother and I always loved "The Garden Song" best. We sang it in the garden as we weeded alongside our parents: "*Inch by inch, row by row . . . Someone bless these seeds I sow. Someone warm them from below 'til the rain comes tumblin' down.*" Not until I had children of my own did I truly understand what the song was about. I remember the day that song started to play as I watched my son toddling across the living room, and my eyes filled with tears as it hit me: it's a metaphor for parenting!

And so it is. Now my own children sing it, and when the song starts to play, our three-year-old yells out, "Hey I know that song! It's 'Seeds I Sow'!" And somehow, that seems like the proper name for the song.

Acknowledgments

MANY PEOPLE have encouraged and helped me as I worked on this book. I am enormously grateful to my amazing editor, Quynh Do, for her incredibly helpful suggestions and feedback throughout the process of working on this book, from the earliest stages of development to its completion. I also thank the outstanding team at W. W. Norton for their work on this book and for the beautiful cover. Special thanks to Drew Weitman for exceptional editorial assistance and Charlotte Kelchner for outstanding copyediting. To my friends, family, and colleagues who read the full manuscript and offered invaluable feedback and encouragement, I thank Heather Daniels, Philip J. Ivanhoe, Michael Puett, Michael Slater, Dorothy Cline, and Kelly Cline. My thanks to the numerous friends whose stories and words inspired me (some of which are included in this book), including Bob and Alice Baird, Kelly Cline and Jamie Harmon, Elisa Hong, Jessica Hennessy, Philip J. Ivanhoe and Hong Jiang, Becky and Tod Linafelt, Amber Lockwood, Amanda Manoel, Joe

Murphy, and Jonathan and Michelle Ray. Thanks to Jim Milward for originally encouraging me to undertake this project. Most importantly, I thank my husband Michael, for making this book possible in too many ways to list, and our children, Patrick, Bridget, and Siobhan, for their remarkable love, inspiration, and wisdom. This book is dedicated to my parents, with all my heart.

Suggestions for Further Reading

TRANSLATIONS OF CHINESE PHILOSOPHERS

Confucius. *Analects: With Selections from Traditional Commentaries*. Translated by Edward Slingerland. Indianapolis, IN: Hackett, 2003. (Translation with selections from traditional Confucian commentaries that help to explain difficult passages.)

Ivanhoe, Philip J., and Bryan W. Van Norden, eds. *Readings in Classical Chinese Philosophy*. Indianapolis, IN: Hackett, 2005. (Anthology with selections from the philosophers I discuss in this book.)

Laozi. *The Daodejing of Laozi*. Translated by Philip J. Ivanhoe. Indianapolis, IN: Hackett, 2003. (Translation of the Daoist classic accompanied by a helpful introduction.)

Mencius. *Mencius*. Translated by Irene Bloom; edited and introduced by Philip J. Ivanhoe. New York: Columbia University Press, 2009. (Translation with a helpful introduction to Mencius's thought and influence in East Asia.)

Mengzi. *Mengzi: With Selections from Traditional Commentaries*. Translated with introduction and notes by Bryan W. Van Norden. Indianapolis, IN: Hackett, 2008. (Translation of Mencius with selections from influential Confucian commentary that explains difficult passages.)

BOOKS ABOUT CHINESE PHILOSOPHY

Ivanhoe, Philip J. *Confucian Reflections: Ancient Wisdom for Modern Times*. New York: Routledge, 2013.

———. *Oneness: East Asian Conceptions of Virtues, Happiness, and How We Are All Connected*. New York: Oxford University Press, 2017.

Puett, Michael. *The Path: What Chinese Philosophers Can Teach Us about the Good Life*. New York: Simon & Schuster, 2016.

Slingerland, Edward. *Trying Not to Try: Ancient China, Modern Science, and the Power of Spontaneity*. New York: Broadway, 2015.

Notes

INTRODUCTION

1. David Mallett, "The Garden Song," *Genius*, https://genius
.com/David-mallett-garden-song-lyrics.
2. Philip J. Ivanhoe, *Confucian Moral Self Cultivation* (Indianapolis, IN: Hackett, 2000).
3. Alison Gopnik, *The Gardener and the Carpenter: What the
New Science of Child Development Tells Us about the Relationship
between Parents and Children* (New York: Farrar, Straus and
Giroux, 2016), 18.
4. Michael Puett and Christine Gross-Loh, *The Path: What
Chinese Philosophers Can Teach Us about the Good Life* (New
York: Simon & Schuster, 2016), 68.
5. Bryan W. Van Norden, *Confucius and the Analects: New Essays*
(New York: Oxford University Press, 2002).

CHAPTER 1: CULTIVATED SPROUTS
AND THE DAO OF RITUALS

1. John Kralik, *A Simple Act of Gratitude: How Learning to Say
Thank You Changed My Life* (New York: Hyperion, 2010).

2. Confucius, "Book Three," 3.4, in *Analects: With Selections from Traditional Commentaries*, trans. Edward Slingerland (Indianapolis, IN: Hackett, 2003).

3. Confucius, *Analects* 3.12, my translation.

4. Confucius, *Analects* 9.3, my translation.

CHAPTER 2: SPROUTS IN NATURE
AND THE DAO OF STICKS

1. Gene Weingarten, "Pearls before Breakfast," *Washington Post*, April 8, 2007.

2. Laozi, "Book One (Chapters 1–37)," chap. 28, in *The Daodejing of Laozi*, trans. Philip J. Ivanhoe (Indianapolis, IN: Hackett, 2003).

3. Laozi, "Book One," chap. 1, in *Daodejing of Laozi*.

4. Laozi, "Book Two (Chapters 38–81)," chap. 55, in *Daodejing of Laozi*.

5. Laozi, "Book One," chap. 28, in *Daodejing of Laozi*.

6. Zhuangzi, "Chapter Nineteen: Mastering Life," in *The Complete Works of Chuang Tzu*, trans. Burton Watson (New York: Columbia University Press, 1968).

7. Laozi, "Book One," chap. 15, in *Daodejing of Laozi*.

8. Laozi, "Book Two," chap. 63, in *Daodejing of Laozi*.

9. Edward Slingerland, *Trying Not to Try* (New York: Broadway Books, 2014), 8.

10. Laozi, "Book One," chap. 20, in *Daodejing of Laozi*.

11. Richard Louv, *Last Child in the Woods: Saving Our Children from Nature-Deficit Disorder* (Chapel Hill, NC: Algonquin Books, 2008).

12. James Taylor, "Copperline," in "James Taylor: My Life in 15 Songs," interview by Andy Greene, *Rolling Stone*, Aug. 20, 2015.

CHAPTER 3: WATCHING SPROUTS GROW:
THE DAO OF MINDFULNESS

1. Confucius, *Analects* 5.16, my translation.
2. Confucius, "Book Four," 4.8, in *Analects: With Selections from Traditional Commentaries*, trans. Edward Slingerland (Indianapolis, IN: Hackett, 2003).
3. Confucius, "Book Fifteen," 15.29, in *Analects: With Selections from Traditional Commentaries*.
4. Confucius, *Analects* 1.2, my translation.
5. Mencius, "Book Four," 4A27, in "Mengzi (Mencius)," trans. Bryan W. Van Norden, in *Readings in Classical Chinese Philosophy*, ed. Philip J. Ivanhoe and Bryan W. Van Norden (Indianapolis, IN: Hackett, 2005).
6. Confucius, *Analects* 6.12, my translation.
7. Confucius, *Analects* 8.7, my translation.
8. Confucius, "Book Six," 6.20, in *Analects: With Selections from Traditional Commentaries*.
9. Confucius, "Book Four," 4.21, in *Analects: With Selections from Traditional Commentaries*.
10. Zhuangzi, "Chapter Five: Signs of Abundant Virtue," in "Zhuangzi," trans. Paul Kjellberg, in *Readings in Classical Chinese Philosophy*.
11. Zhuangzi, "Chapter Thirteen: Heaven's Way," in *Readings in Classical Chinese Philosophy*.
12. Laozi, "Book Two (Chapters 38–81)," chap. 80, in *The Daodejing of Laozi*, trans. Philip J. Ivanhoe (Indianapolis, IN: Hackett, 2003).
13. Laozi, "Book Two," chap. 63, in *Daodejing of Laozi*.
14. Laozi, "Book Two," chap. 48, in *Daodejing of Laozi*.
15. Laozi, "Book Two," chap. 52, in *Daodejing of Laozi*.
16. Laozi, "Book Two," chap. 63, in *Daodejing of Laozi*.
17. Laozi, "Book Two," chap. 63, in *Daodejing of Laozi*.

18. Laozi, "Book One," chap. 11, in *Daodejing of Laozi*.
19. Zhuangzi, "Chapter Two: On Equalizing Things," in *Readings in Classical Chinese Philosophy*.
20. Confucius, *Analects* 19.7, my translation.

CHAPTER 4: UPROOTED SPROUTS
AND THE DAO OF LEARNING

1. *Mencius*, "Chapter Two," 2A2, my translation.
2. Andrea Orr, "Unschooling: What Is It and How One Family Does It," *Washington Post*, February 25, 2015.
3. Michael S. Roth, "You Didn't Get into Harvard, So What?," review of *Where You Go Is Not Who You'll Be*, by Frank Bruni, *Washington Post*, April 10, 2015.
4. Confucius, *Analects* 4.5, my translation.
5. Confucius, *Analects* 1.16, my translation.
6. Confucius, "Book Seven," 7.16, in *Analects: With Selections from Traditional Commentaries, trans. Edward Slingerland* (Indianapolis, IN: Hackett, 2003).
7. Jessica Lahey, "Why Kids Care More about Achievement than Helping Others: A New Study Suggests that Parents and Teachers May Be Sending Kids the Wrong Message," *The Atlantic*, June 25, 2014.
8. *Mencius*, "Chapter Six," 6A15, my translation.
9. *Zhuangzi*, "Chapter Two: On Equalizing Things," in "Zhuangzi," trans. Paul Kjellberg, in *Readings in Classical Chinese Philosophy*, ed. Philip J. Ivanhoe and Bryan W. Van Norden (Indianapolis, IN: Hackett, 2005).
10. Ari Brown, *Toddler 411* (Boulder, CO: Windsor Peak Press, 2009).
11. *Mencius*, "Book Six," 6A8, in *Readings in Classical Chinese Philosophy*.

12. Confucius, *Analects* 2.15, in *Confucian Moral Self Cultivation*, trans. Philip J. Ivanhoe (Indianapolis, IN: Hackett, 2000).

13. Confucius, "Book One," 1.7, in *Analects: With Selections from Traditional Commentaries*.

14. Confucius, "Book Six," 6.3, in *Analects: With Selections from Traditional Commentaries*.

15. Confucius, "Book Seventeen," 17.8, in *Analects: With Selections from Traditional Commentaries*.

CHAPTER 5: SPROUTS, NOT SEEDS:
THE DAO OF NATURE AND NURTURE

1. Paul Bloom, *Just Babies: The Origins of Good and Evil* (New York: Broadway, 2013).

2. Philip J. Ivanhoe, *Confucian Reflections: Ancient Wisdom for Modern Times* (New York: Routledge, 2013).

3. Mencius, "Book Two," 2A6, in "Mengzi (Mencius)," trans. Bryan W. Van Norden, in *Readings in Classical Chinese Philosophy*, ed. Philip J. Ivanhoe and Bryan W. Van Norden (Indianapolis, IN: Hackett, 2005).

4. Mencius, "Book Two," 2A6, in *Readings in Classical Chinese Philosophy*.

5. Bryan W. Van Norden, *Introduction to Classical Chinese Philosophy* (Indianapolis, IN: Hackett, 2011).

6. Mencius, "Book Two," 2A6, in *Readings in Classical Chinese Philosophy*.

7. Mencius, "Book Six," 6A6, in *Readings in Classical Chinese Philosophy*.

8. Mencius, "Book Six," 6A7, in *Readings in Classical Chinese Philosophy*.

9. Xunzi, "Chapter Twenty-Three: Human Nature Is Bad," in

"Xunzi," trans. Eric L. Hutton, in *Readings in Classical Chinese Philosophy*.

10. Xunzi, "Chapter Two: Cultivating Oneself," in *Readings in Classical Chinese Philosophy*.

11. Xunzi, "Chapter Twenty-Three: Human Nature Is Bad," in *Readings in Classical Chinese Philosophy*.

12. Xunzi, "Chapter One: An Exhortation to Learning," in *Readings in Classical Chinese Philosophy*.

13. Xunzi, "Chapter Nineteen: Discourse on Ritual" and "Chapter Twenty-Three: Human Nature Is Bad," in *Readings in Classical Chinese Philosophy*.

14. Bloom, *Just Babies*, 7–8.

15. Martin Hoffman, *Empathy and Moral Development* (New York: Cambridge University Press, 2000).

16. Xunzi, "Chapter One: An Exhortation to Learning," in *Readings in Classical Chinese Philosophy*.

17. Angela Duckworth, *Grit: The Power of Passion and Perseverance* (New York: Scribner, 2016).

18. Duckworth, *Grit*; see also Paul Tough, *How Children Succeed* (New York: Mariner Books, 2012).

19. Tough, *How Children Succeed*, 84.

20. Michael Jordan "Failure" Nike commercial, 1997, https://www.youtube.com/watch?v=45mMioJ5szc.

21. Tough, *How Children Succeed*, 165.

22. Sarah Gardner, "Growth Mindset Ways to Help Your Child," 2015, https://www.teacherspayteachers.com/Product/Growth-Mindset-FREEBIE-1988801.

23. Laozi, "Book Two (Chapters 38–81)," chap. 63, in *The Daodejing of Laozi*, trans. Philip J. Ivanhoe (Indianapolis, IN: Hackett, 2003).

24. Anne Lamott, *Bird by Bird: Some Instructions on Writing and Life* (New York: Anchor Books, 1995).

25. Xunzi, "Chapter One: An Exhortation to Learning," in *Readings in Classical Chinese Philosophy*.

CHAPTER 6: THE LITTLEST SPROUT:
THE DAO OF DISABILITIES AND CHALLENGES

1. *Mencius,* "Chapter Six," 6A15, my translation.
2. Karen Carr and Philip J. Ivanhoe, *The Sense of Antirationalism: The Religious Thought of Zhuangzi and Kierkegaard* (CreateSpace, 2010), 51.
3. Zhuangzi, "Chapter Three: The Key to Nourishing Life," in "Zhuangzi," trans. Paul Kjellberg, in *Readings in Classical Chinese Philosophy*, ed. Philip J. Ivanhoe and Bryan W. Van Norden (Indianapolis, IN: Hackett, 2005).
4. Eric Schwitzgebel, "Skill and Disability in Zhuangzi," *The Splintered Mind* (blog), Sept. 10, 2014, http://schwitzsplinters .blogspot.com/2014/09/skill-and-disability-in-zhuangzi .html.
5. Zhuangzi, "Chapter Four: The Human Realm," in *Readings in Classical Chinese Philosophy*.
6. Zhuangzi, "Chapter Five: Signs of Abundant Virtue," in *Readings in Classical Chinese Philosophy*.
7. Timothy Shriver, *Fully Alive: Discovering What Matters Most* (New York: Sarah Crichton Books, 2014).
8. Raun Kaufman, *Autism Breakthrough* (New York: St. Martin's Press, 2014), 80.
9. Zhuangzi, "Chapter Three: The Key to Nourishing Life," in *Readings in Classical Chinese Philosophy*.
10. Zhuangzi, "Chapter Six: The Great Ancestral Teacher," in *Readings in Classical Chinese Philosophy*.
11. Zhuangzi, "Chapter Six: The Great Ancestral Teacher," in *Readings in Classical Chinese Philosophy*.
12. Zhuangzi, "Chapter Six: The Great Ancestral Teacher," in *Readings in Classical Chinese Philosophy*.
13. Alvin Powell, "Search until You Find a Passion and Go All Out to Excel in Its Expression," *Harvard Gazette*, Apr. 15, 2014.

14. Temple Grandin, *Thinking in Pictures: My Life with Autism* (New York: Vintage Books, 2006), 168–69.

15. Oliver Sacks, foreword to *Thinking in Pictures*, by Temple Grandin, xviii.

16. Grandin, *Thinking in Pictures*, 50.

17. *The Address*, written and directed by Ken Burns (Walpole, NH: Florentine Films, 2014).

18. Zhuangzi, "Chapter Four: The Human Realm," in *Readings in Classical Chinese Philosophy*.

19. Zhuangzi, "Chapter One: Wandering Round and About," in *Readings in Classical Chinese Philosophy*.

CHAPTER 7: FROM SPROUT TO PLANT:
THE DAO OF VOCATION

1. Barbara Cooney, *Miss Rumphius* (New York: Puffin Books, 1985).

2. Philip J. Ivanhoe, *Oneness: East Asian Conceptions of Happiness, Virtue, and How We Are All Connected* (New York: Oxford University Press, 2017).

3. Zhuangzi, "Chapter Three: The Key to Nourishing Life," in "Zhuangzi," trans. Paul Kjellberg, in *Readings in Classical Chinese Philosophy*, ed. Philip J. Ivanhoe and Bryan W. Van Norden (Indianapolis, IN: Hackett, 2005).

4. Zhuangzi, "Chapter Nineteen: Mastering Life," in *The Complete Works of Chuang Tzu*, trans. Burton Watson (New York: Columbia University Press, 1968).

5. Zhuangzi, "Chapter Seven: The Proper Way for Emperors and Kings," in *Readings in Classical Chinese Philosophy*.

6. Deborah Shepherd-Hayes, *A Guide for Using* The Mouse and the Motorcycle *in the Classroom* (Teacher Created Resources, 1996), 6.

7. Zhuangzi, "Chapter Thirteen: Heaven's Way," in *Readings in Classical Chinese Philosophy*.

8. Michael S. Roth, "You Didn't Get into Harvard, So What?," review of *Where You Go Is Not Who You'll Be*, by Frank Bruni, *Washington Post*, Apr. 10, 2015.

9. Paul Tough, *How Children Succeed* (New York: Mariner Books, 2012), xv.

10. Richard Louv, *Last Child in the Woods: Saving Our Children from Nature-Deficit Disorder* (Chapel Hill, NC: Algonquin Books, 2008), 72.

11. Petula Dvorak, "Little Bro Teaches This Family Some Life Lessons," *Washington Post*, Jan. 1, 2018.

Index

About the Author

ERIN CLINE is professor of comparative ethics at Georgetown University, where she teaches in the departments of theology and philosophy as well as the Asian Studies Program, and is a Senior Research Fellow in the Berkley Center for Religion, Peace, and World Affairs. She is the author of three books and more than twenty research articles on Chinese philosophy and comparative philosophy and religion, including *Families of Virtue: Confucian and Western Views on Childhood Development*. She lives in Maryland with her husband and three children.